GET YOUR MIND RIGHT

THINK OUTSIDE THE BOX

KNOW YOU'RE IN ONE

JUSTICE

Get Your Mind Right

By Kenneth Wyche

An Imprint of Kenneth Wyche Publishing

To the person who inspired this book.

CHAPTER 1

Get Your Mind Right

Getting your mind right means adjusting your thinking. The brain is malleable. You can adapt and change. Thought revision is a core theme in higher aspects of life, often depicted in religious texts like the Bible. The word "repent" literally means "change your mind." Getting your mind right is changing your mind in the correct direction. "Right" has some subjectivity, however, utilize this operational definition when deciphering "right" in this context: that which is most relevant to your alignment.

Alignment refers to your positioning in relation to yourself. Are you confident in yourself, do you believe in yourself, and are you aware of your transmuted identity? You are a spiritual being having a physical experience. Alignment is living in harmony with yourself and operating from that place of revelation. So, are you operating from a paradigm of thought that supports your authenticity, or one that refutes it?

One of the biggest deceptions that can fall upon a person is having a lack of willingness to believe in oneself. Willpower or exertion is reliant on your convictions. If you're not convicted about or by it, you're probably not motivated about or by it either. With conviction comes meaning and purpose. What you are willing to struggle for is what matters to you.

People have lost the will to struggle for the essence of life. Struggle is a critical component of human existence. Jesus struggled in the wilderness for 40 days and 40 nights before he started his ministry. Before you arrive, you must get to; and to get to [your proverbial destination] you must go through.

In general people have ceded ground on what matters to them because they have become uninspired to endure for improvement. Improvement can be anything, social, personal, professional, or otherwise. If you are unwilling to fight against the challenges that arise when you persevere hardships for a desired end, you'll vacillate in your ability to self-actualize. Ceding ground in this way is like leaving money on the table in the form of unrealized potential and undiscovered meaning and purpose.

A graveyard is the richest place on earth due to it holding a slew of unfulfilled dreams and possibilities. People don't see the fullness of their desires because they are not willing to strive for them. Progress is a proactive activity. If you want to get better, you must do better. Doing better is hard; so instead of doing better people look for another solution or a path of least resistance.

It's like subsidized foods. Historically healthy foods aren't the ones that receive subsidy. But just because an unhealthy food is more affordable doesn't mean it's the right choice. It's right here where getting your mind right is required: in the choices you make that have an impact on your life. It's not enough to change your mind if you're changing your mind in a harmful way. Changing your mind yields more fruitful results for your quality of life when you are doing so inspired by a [operationally defined] "right" decision.

The word "desire" has Latin roots that mean "of-the-Father." "De" means "of" and "sidus" or "sidere" where the word "sire" comes from, refers to being "from the stars." Sire is a male parent or father. The word "father" in this context therefore refers to a paternal [like] being from the cosmos.

A desire is something you get from a star like father aka God. It doesn't matter how you acknowledge spiritual influence in your life, the fact is it's there. Whether he's God the father to you, or the universe, or something else, the point is your desires are divinely imbued. And God wouldn't have put them in you if they were not meant to be fulfilled through you. But you've got to want it. If the God of the universe gave you desires influenced by himself, that he wants to manifest in your life, what else do you think he could have given you?

How you get your mind to consider that which is most relevant to your alignment is by embracing who you are and embracing your context. Again, the essence of life is antithetical to the trajectory of life. Part of life is trial and tribulation, yet people are constantly trying to solve for pain. But sometimes the pain isn't meant to be solved, it's meant to be endured. Because the reality of the situation is, not all pain is life threatening, some is just uncomfortable. Generally speaking, you're not in danger if something doesn't go exactly the way you want it.

Life can be scary, but it isn't meant to be. Life wants to happen for you not to you. God uses life to shape and mold you. When you come up against struggles and difficulties in life, your reality isn't the problem, your thinking is. Getting your mind right is about maximizing your potential within your context. The word "potential" means the spectrum of your possibilities, or in another word, nothing. Everyone has the potential to be anything, the differentiator in realizing the fullness of your potential is in identifying, aligning, and making decisions that are geared towards the actualization of your authentic self and God given desires.

When you get your mind right you can make decisions about your reality (the things you live with every day you wake up) that are self-serving and circumstance improving, as opposed to self-deprecating and circumstance exasperating. You don't have to change and become someone you're not just because who you are is not producing the results you'd like. Getting your mind right in this context looks like improving yourself not altering yourself (though in some scenarios alterations may be appropriate as well).

The fullness of you shows up when you tap into your authenticity. People are afraid to be authentic because vulnerability can lead to getting hurt, and society teaches us to again, solve for pain. This can cause people to respond to the fear of being hurt somewhere vulnerable by choosing an easy out and being someone disingenuous. The easy way isn't always the right way, especially if the easy way causes you to capitulate on your values, have a dilapidated hope, and or starve your desires. The struggles in your life are there to shape you; think about them differently. Instead of always solving for pain figure out a way to get stronger from it and better endure it. This is the type of mindset and thought process required to get your mind right.

CHAPTER 2

How to Create the Life you Want

Are you tired? Have the negative things of life had the last laugh at every pivotal point? Are you disgruntled at your job, in your relationships, with the state of the world? Now more than ever the opportunity to be the person you have always wanted to be is manifesting all around you.

The thing keeping you from where you want to be is your mindset. Here is a simple trick on how to change your life and create your ideal reality:

Change your mind, Change your life.

Yup. That's it. No long-elaborate bullet points or top five hacks. Simply, change your mind, change your life.

During the Covid-19 pandemic I got very into

mentorship. At the same time the riots of 2020 were taking place. And as people took to the streets on behalf of the injustices done to people who looked like me, at the time, I became emboldened. Around this time is when a friend of mine also taught me a valuable lesson on the power of mental fortitude and determination.

I was experiencing a metamorphosis.

Hindsight is 20/20 and while I may not have said that then, I realize now that foundation was being laid for me to become something greater. I was a bum around the pandemic. Fresh out of graduate school with no prospects, laid off from a job that I knew wasn't for me long-term anyway, and surviving off family contributions.

I needed to do something with my life.

When Covid-19 took full swing in the summer of 2020 I as well as I believe a lot of people had a realization. Mine was that I can start working on myself, growing, and developing. Through prayer and guidance, I applied my faith to something I truly didn't understand. All I knew was convention wasn't for me and that Covid-19 presented an opportunity for me to do something about it. That's when I realized that life is what you make of it, literally.

Manifestation

This is where the concept of manifestation entered my life. During and since the pandemic, I have had the opportunity to engage in "thought therapy," and I have put myself in alignment with the life that I want.

What does that mean, you may be asking? It means that I learned how to stop fighting against life, and against myself. I have become a co-creator of my life and not just someone along for the ride. I say co-creator because of the serendipitous and non-controllable aspects of life.

To do this for yourself you have to start with your mindset. Are your thoughts in alignment with your situation, or your desires?

When you know what you want-you know what you want. Your circumstances, however, can be on a constant swivel. The strength of your mindset is in how tenaciously it allows you to cling onto your desires, and not to or despite of your circumstances.

The Law of Attraction

The Law of Attraction is described as: the ability to manifest or materialize (make real) into your life whatever you are focusing on. It's the idea that you are and can have what you think.

Maybe you have heard of and or intentionally or unintentionally engaged with the law of attraction before. And maybe you have done so in a way that may not have yielded ideal results. The Bible says that life and death are in the power of the tongue. I used to speak very negatively over myself, friends and family, romantic relationships, my career path, and more.

What you need to realize is, what gets repeated gets remembered, and what gets remembered gets done. There wasn't much of any subjectively (as it pertains to me) objectively (without question and not up for debate) meaningful or positive fruit (results or outcomes) in those areas of my life, because I kept affirming (engaging my confirmation bias) to myself that I was not worthy of my desires in those specific areas of my life (I elaborate more on this from a different perspective in Chapter 22). Habits and behavioral patterns like the one being described (speaking negatively) can proliferate and metastasize to other areas of your life. What you articulate is what emanates from your heart. What you speak is who you are, and you take you with you everywhere you go. Subsequently you have influence over the nouns (people, places, and things) in your life simply by how you talk to and or about them.

Thought change is heart change. Your heart from an objective perspective is an organ. Your heart from a conceptual perspective is the amalgamation and manifestation of your essence. "Your essence" from a behavioral perspective stem from your temperament, personality, proclivities, and character. Who you are, while fundamental to your lived experience is also malleable. From a biological and scientific perspective your mind is malleable and not just for the first 25 years of your life. Certain scientific studies have found that your brain can grow, adapt, and change over the course of your entire life. When you change your mind, you change your heart. This doesn't mean you change what makes you unique. That aspect of yourself experiences maturation and undergoes development with the passage of time. What changes is how you conduct yourself (behave) within the context of your understanding of yourself.

Who you are influences what you do and what you do influences who you are. It's a positive feedback loop in terms of influence not outcome. The chicken must come before the egg. The creator makes the created. That is what your heart is, the proverbial chicken or metaphorical creator of what you experience regardless of the connotations of whatever circumstantial evidence you may or may not have.

With respect to these concepts and the struggles I had, I was also engaging with those areas of my life maladaptively, or in a way out of alignment, or with a corrupt(ed) heart and mind, that didn't truly represent what I wanted (the matters of the heart can be complicated because while all humans have the capacity for evil there are some people who lean into being evil, while others strive to be good, while yet and still others vacillate somewhere in between). Simply put, some of what you go through isn't your fault and the reality of this revelation can be devastating for a host of reasons.

Effective application of the law of attraction looks like shifting your subconscious and allowing your expectations to create your reality (allowing what's inside of you to come forth throughout your lived experience). Once I shifted my focus from my circumstances to my desires, I put myself in and on the path of what I really want. The more you advance in your understanding of life the more the semantics of life matter.

The Law of Vibration

Everything has its own vibrational frequency. Everything around us at a molecular level is in constant motion. Even stationary and or solid objects are in constant motion, vibrating molecularly at a higher frequency creating the perception and experience of density or being dense.

Since everything vibrates on a molecular level, including humans, because of our thoughts and emotions, we are essentially frequency conductors. You manifest in the now whatever is attracted to you based on whatever frequency you're on. And the way you modulate that frequency is through your thoughts and emotions.

Have you ever wanted something so bad, and one day the right opportunity came along seemingly out of nowhere? What you were doing was raising your vibrations to be in alignment with that thing you wanted.

Around 42% of people are more likely to complete their goals when they write them down. This is a pragmatic practice of manifestation. When you get on the same vibrational frequency as what you want, you put yourself in a position for it to actually manifest-materialize-be made plain or solid.

The key or trick to this is to know what you want, which I can attest to as sometimes being a challenge to decipher. One of the things that can make it challenging is dramatization. Sometimes you can be put in a situation where the clarity of what you want is muddied by yours or someone else's intentions for you to make emotional or over sensationalized decisions. Sometimes you can be gaslit into insanity because you or some noun around you wants you to for lack of a better phrase make a mountain out of a mole hill. What you want doesn't always have to be deep, philosophical, or existential.

Sometimes when that happens to you, you are being confused (made to become corrupted or maladapted). Whoever the perpetrator of this kind of confusion is, isn't inherently doing this for your best interest. Some people may not want you to realize what you actually want because what you actually want may not be them. And you may not want to face what you actually want because what you actually want may not be what you've committed a certain aspect of your life to up to this point. What you really want may likely be more conceptually ethereal, than superficial. While what is superficial is nice and generally a good outcome, it can also be a distraction from what really matters.

An Attractive Mindset

Your biggest obstacle is your mind, and your confirmation bias is your Achilles hill. If you can learn to think better, you will become better. By training yourself to affirm better thoughts you create the space for a better reality to materialize.

This happens because during the transmutation process from thought to thing your thoughts take on their attributes in the form of the thing(s) vibrating at the same vibrational frequency as themselves (your thought's vibrational frequency). When you materialize something, you are dragging into the physical dimension something which has up to that point been primarily ethereal for you. Another word for this is faith.

Faith is the substance of things hoped for and the evidence of things not seen. Whatever becomes substance or matter in your life, was likely (though not always, things can have a unique nature about themselves) ethereal or at least a thought first.

The challenge with thinking better is that it requires you to change how you think about what you think, also referred to as your default thinking.

That thing that you think about when you are not thinking must change; because that is what determines the trajectory of your life.

Your subconscious drives you, and your confirmation bias is the GPS. Your confirmation bias is your ability to favor information that affirms what you already believe or understand to be true. Human biology and psychology are inclined to gravitate towards things that affirm what we already believe because, fundamentally there is at least a perception of safety in the familiar. Safety from a psychological and biological perspective is objectively how you prolong your life, of which most if not all living things have an innate desire to do. This is also known as the will to live.

An example of confirmation bias is if you have ever wanted a certain type of car before or had just purchased a new one; and all the sudden you start seeing that car all around your neighborhood. This happens because your mind looks for things in and around your life that affirm what you believe. In this example, that affirmed belief lends itself to you feeling safe by reinforcing your decision to want or buy that kind of car. "It must be at least a decent car if not a good one if I keep seeing several people with it." That's how your confirmation bias fortifies various aspects of your consciousness and identity formation. You can willfully engage in this process when you make concrete decisions about what you want.

Despite the name, your confirmation bias is relatively objective. You can affirm either positive or negative thoughts and cause them to perpetuate in your mind. Every day you shape your reality because you are naturally drawn to- attract to yourself what you already believe, reinforcing that notion, good or bad, in your life.

Can You Believe Better?

The real question of all of this is, can you believe better? The answer is yes, but it takes effort. The healthier or more positive or more in alignment the thought and emotion, the better your materialized result will be. What you believe or your core morals or values is one of the main contributing factors to how you think. The drawback to believing in something is that there will always be opposition to that belief. What you choose to focus on should be set with clear intentions. You need to know what you want and why you want it as if it is already yours.

If you can be resolute in what you believe the opposition does not matter, because you are focused; and that thing that you are focused on is being affirmed in your life every single day.

Your circumstance may tell you that you can't have what you want, but what you believe must be truer than what you see or hear. You can't allow the noise of the world to drown out your desires. This isn't reality denialism, it's choosing to decide to do something about your reality and once concluding on what that something is, being committed to that decision and course of action. Once you are there and if you follow what's outlined in this chapter, the rest will begin to happen naturally. Which in effect, is the whole point.

CHAPTER 3

Win or Die Trying

Humans have needs. We need shelter, clothing, and sustenance. Where do you think those things come from? Resources. Resources are acquired. How do you acquire resources? They have to be taken. Through evolution humans have civilized the hunting and gathering process by rewarding certain behaviors over others. The need never changed, the means of acquiring the need did.

Instead of foraging for fruits, nuts, seeds, killing wild beasts, and catching fish, we perform. We've turned intellect and means of production into something more valuable than the product itself. This is a perversion because people live off the product. It's the product that fuels and covers you in a literal sense. Your ability to attain the product isn't as important as the product itself, especially when you don't have the ability to attain it.

People will sell millions of dollars' worth of bad product(s) but get rewarded for their ability to do so. On the other hand, not all products are bad, and they contribute greatly to the advancement of society. Though often those societal advancements are exploited for even more money or profit, with little return to the people who directly contribute to the innovation, and often at the expense of your ability to continue to be able to provide for yourself.

Then there are premium products, or products that may or may not be essential, but they have a price tag that suggests otherwise, pricing certain people out of being able to afford that particular good or service. *Have you ever considered what you give up by not producing anything for yourself?* Money isn't a fundamental need, it's a means to a need and more. Be in the middle of nowhere, with no means of transportation, no way to get in contact with anyone, and no one ever coming to rescue you in a material way; with a fist full of cash and little to no hard or survival skills and tell me how warm that money will keep you when the sun goes down. How safe it will keep you when the wild animals start roaming, or how full it will keep your stomach.

When you don't have the product/resource, and cannot get it for yourself, you are losing evolutionarily. If you don't have money and don't know where or how to get any, that's a problem. If money ever goes obsolete and you don't know how or aren't resourceful enough to make sure you and your family are still able to eat and keep warm at night, you are losing. People have been robbed of their survival skills.

Civilization is only civil if it works. You need to ensure that you're anarchy proof. This isn't fear mongering, this is science. Survival of the fittest is a scientific concept. Again, this goes both ways. How are you generating revenue for yourself? Do you have multiple streams of income? Are you retaining value from your labor? Is your money working for you? And or do you have a hard skill? If you're not at least thinking about any of the aforementioned, you're losing at life. Survival is fluid. It's not what you're surviving, it's that you're surviving. It's not a choice. It's a bare minimum.

Some of us have to endure some difficult things and I empathize with that, but the drive of life is that you survive. Life wants you to survive it. Life respects longevity. God wants to see you make it to the end of your life. You can't die prematurely. That means you also can't give up either. At some point you have to make a choice, win or die trying. You're going to die anyway. Everyone dies. Are you going to die choosing to do nothing? Or are you going to tap into what's inside of you, find that drive and will to live, and go make it happen!?

CHAPTER 4

Doing the Right Thing in the Wrong Place

Have you ever felt like your efforts were fruitless? No matter how hard you work, regardless of the fact that you always show up, and indifferent to you doing the morally right thing, your circumstances refuse to improve and, in some cases, may have gotten worse. In these situations, it can be a common thought to just work harder.

When you are failing to bend life to your will the widely shared insight is that you are either doing something wrong, or you're not doing enough. Sometimes you may put that burden on yourself and think that if you could increase productivity then maybe something will turn in your favor. The issue with this line of thinking is not everything you suffer through is your fault and sometimes it's not your work that will save you, but rather a miracle.

One of the things people can struggle with is the relinquishing of control. You can work against yourself when you try too hard. I'm not saying that you shouldn't try to affect change; I'm saying when you're trying to affect change and change isn't materializing for you, then it may be time to take a different approach. Doing the right thing in the wrong place suggests that you aren't the problem, your context is.

The things of your life are holding you back. This could be anything from the people you associate with, the places you live, work, and spend time, and or your extracurricular activities. Something about your circumstance is barren. Something in your life isn't functioning correctly. You don't need to work harder; you need to relocate. Someone in life is in a similar contextual situation as you are right now, and they are thriving (not saying you're not, but to make a point).

How can the same or similar set of conditions produce one thing for one person, and something else for another? It's the where. The place is bad. A good way to paint this picture is with soil. When you plant, generally speaking, you want to do so with good soil. You want the ground to be healthy and the dirt to be nutrient rich. Your life has a strong correlation with this analogy. If the proverbial, metaphorical, and or literal ground you are required to derive sustenance from is bad, then it doesn't matter how hard you work, bad ground won't produce, produce.

What complicates this whole thing is the gap that can present itself between knowing there is a problem and being able to do something about it. What I am sharing with you here may not be new to you. Maybe you've known for a while that your situation is malfunctioning to say the least. The problem is either you don't know what to do about it, or there isn't much that you can do about it. Sure you'd pack up and move to a different state or country tomorrow if those stars aligned and it made sense. But sometimes the same thing that is the problem, is the same thing blocking your solution.

If you were just able to get a better job things would improve, but a better job has been elusive for the better half of the last half decade. Maybe you don't live near family and if you were just closer to them at least you would have a support system; but getting to family can be a herculean task of proximity both in terms of physical distance and sometimes mental and emotional distance as well. These are real life issues that a lack of resources can create for you. When you don't own the means to take things into your own hands, and your access to the resources themselves are limited, you are in an unfortunate situation.

This is where tenacity comes in. Get creative with your problem solving. The facts on the ground will remain the same until they change. You need a quality-of-life improvement whether it be personally, financially, socially, geographically, or otherwise. If you can't do that for yourself then you need to figure out what you can do to usher yourself up to a breakthrough. A breakthrough is an opportunity or revelation that has the potential to change your life for the better.

It's a thing that allows for other things to change. It's an unexpected call you get from an old friend or coworker offering you a new position. It's that bright idea that gives you a new approach to something. It's your hobby that turns into a business. It's an influx of cash and or the absolving of a responsibility. A breakthrough can come in various forms. The point of it, however, is to give you a chance to make a change. The way you usher yourself to a breakthrough moment is by putting yourself in a position for a breakthrough to happen.

Look at your situation objectively. What would you like to happen? What needs to happen? And what is the most likely to happen? As well as what are all your options? Don't work harder in an unfruitful situation. Figure out how to mitigate greed/stubbornness, and or cut your losses. Understand what your last resort is and uncover whether it's a feasible option. Don't remain ineffectual. Pray. Seek counsel. Give yourself an ultimatum and a deadline. "If this or that doesn't change then this is how I will respond." Conclusively, do what you need to do to make your life worth living.

The problem with remaining inadequate is if you are someone who needs a reason to live, doing nothing with your life is far from helpful. The byproduct of not living meaningfully can be detrimental. Lacking purpose or meaning could negatively impact your mental health from the perspective of depression, mood changes, anxiety, and or suicidal ideations. If you are currently struggling with any of these, seek help immediately. The definition of insanity is doing the same thing over and over and expecting something different from the otherwise consistent result(s). If the same result(s) you keep getting from your efforts is driving you mad, then you need to find refuge. Living in a place of unfulfillment is not a long-term survival strategy.

CHAPTER 5

Don't Waste your Breath

Some things are better left unsaid. Not because they are not of value, but because no one is listening. Have you ever been in a situation where you are speaking to someone and you can see their eyes glaze over, or you can hear a lack of interest in their response? People can get accustomed to hearing themselves speak, while other people can tend to gravitate towards things that confirm their biases.

If you are not saying things to a person that align with their ideology, that experience can devolve into you speaking to a brick wall. Not everyone values or wants to hear what you have to say. The good news is their lack of interest and or receptivity doesn't hinder your ability to share what's been provoked in you to. This is where conflict can emerge. Sometimes regardless of someone else's rigidity you're still called to speak up or say something anyway. When you live in an authentic manner, sometimes what's on your mind isn't what's circulating in the general zeitgeist at that time.

This is an intellectual conflict. What you do well and what you don't, can provide insight for you as to what your purpose is in life, and or in specific contexts. You must know what your role is in a situation and how you can aid in the betterment thereof. Understanding your role on the fly, if you will, comes from having self-awareness and a general grasp on your capabilities. Not every situation you are in will call for you to try to win hearts and minds.

Sometimes the best way to be present is to be silent. Don't underestimate yourself or your contributions, but at the same time if it looks like things are going nowhere fast when you're talking to a person or group, don't dwell on the point. No one is listening. There are caveats here like, in some cases people are listening, but they may be doing so with malicious intent. In those and similar scenarios it's better to keep things brief as well.

More generally I am referring to volunteered information. If you are compensated or required in some capacity to speak, then that requires the gumption to press through respectfully. But in cases of speaking with friends, colleagues, loved ones, groups, and the like, in most of those instances the orator has the luxury of withholding information.

CHAPTER 6

Privilege

In early history it was common for people to live in small units. These small units were families or villages. In this dynamic of human relationships, of which is widely considered to be the ideal or peak form of human existence, people related to each other primarily if not exclusively in an egalitarian way. Egalitarianism is an ideology and approach to politics that espouses that all people are equal and are inherently entitled to equal rights and opportunities. People who lived (and live, there are people who still live like this today) in these villages or nano-civilizations generally shared everything from responsibilities, to resources, to power. All of this changed some 12,000 years ago due to what is sometimes referred to as the Holocene or sixth mass extinction, this one being caused by humans.

    12,000 years ago, is significant because that is when

several scientists agree that agriculture as a means of survival became widespread. Because of various environmental changes across planet earth, agriculture became the most feasible way for people to feed themselves as opposed to hunting and gathering, which while preferable, isn't as sustainable or plentiful as harvesting crops. We're going to go on a bit of a journey to get to the thrust of this chapter, which is, you should handle your privilege with humility.

Privilege is a granted right-something you are allowed to do. Because you are you or are part of a certain group you have the privilege to do "XYZ." In law, a privilege is revocable. If something can be taken away from you, that generally means that you don't own it.

It can be easy to take privilege for granted. There can be a tinge of entitlement that comes with privilege. This is why being humble is the other side of the same coin when discussing this topic. The ideological roots of privilege are in egalitarianism. An unchecked sense of entitlement in virtually any scenario can erode group cohesion. Group cohesion is the immaterial bonds shared among different individuals who are united in pursuing a specific goal or goals. Group cohesion matters because forming a group is how people have evolved to survive. In addition to humans being social beings, groups lend themselves better than isolation to individual survival. For a group to remain unified however, there must be some form of egalitarianism.

Egalitarianism is an outward demonstration of our inner endowment of equality, simply on the fact of being a living organism. Because you exist period, you have rights and you have the right to experience those rights, especially if not definitely within the context of a group where those rights are generally more restrained, to proliferate equality among all members of the group. Less rights for you means more rights for everyone else, which in theory is okay when those collective rights are equal and fair for all. Intentionally or unintentionally exhibiting behaviors that destroy that fabric makes a person maladapted and corrupt from a self-actualization perspective. While ultimately, it's your choice, that is not the kind of person you want to be if you want to experience the fullness of what life has to offer you. Being corrupted will only get you so far. When you exhibit the characteristics and behaviors of positive self- actualization, the sky is the limit. I want to help you live from a place of what could be. When you live in the realm of possibilities, anything becomes possible for you.

Your context enables your privilege. Privilege is a feature or facet of humanity as a species thriving. What you're allowed to get away with (put loosely) in certain contexts may be different than what someone else can. Privilege often presents itself in a hierarchy. The reason it does this is because of the foundational structure of privilege. Hierarchies are a natural occurrence in biology. They help living organisms organize and (or in order to) survive. From a biological perspective hierarchies check off most if not all the survival boxes. There is cooperation, competition and domination, responsibilities, procreation, status, and safety and protection.

One of the happy problems humanity has faced throughout history is surplus. When you grow crops (or make almost anything for that matter) the end product tends to include excess. I am skimming the surface of several topics and areas of study that you should certainly do your own research on if your interest is piqued.

When living in small groups and hunting and gathering becomes unviable for various peoples for one reason or another, those groups and peoples will come together to form one or more larger groups. That process is likely to not be completely symbiotic and because of that, for all the good that comes from that kind of structural reorganization and unification, one glaring challenge that also comes with it is inequality.

In addition to the innate hierarchy of a group (a group is naturally organized whether it be parent and child, leader and subordinate, public servant and citizen, so on and so forth), agriculture-based civilizations create the environment for the accumulation of wealth. The accumulation of wealth, land, food, currency, and various other resources creates another form of hierarchy, one based on materials and the power associated with them. This creates inequality because from the hoarding of wealth comes disparity in the form of the haves and the have nots. Those with less individually, historically must band together and fight for the retention and expansion of their rights. This isn't as much of a thing in a hunting and gathering society because of the reality of those conditions and the dynamics at play. So, even in a condition where hierarchies may exist, in a smaller group it's likely to be more decentralized and therefore more people experience the fullness of their rights.

When people started turning to agriculture as our main food supply, it disconnected us from nature in a visceral way. Speaking generally, people lost their sense of egalitarianism. Helping someone else, to a certain degree, made no sense when God forbid a disaster, you can retain and use your resources for yourself. Because of this common understanding of what is required to survive, hierarchies began to form. Hierarchies stratify privilege and suggest that certain individuals have more rights than others based mainly on their accumulation of stuff. Humanity's sense of egalitarianism took a back seat to survival. The sense of survival of the fittest gave way to the experience of privilege. In your lived experience today, knowing what explicit and or implicit privileges you have enables you to better navigate your life. Being considerate of how you experience your privilege is how you can improve your quality of life, contribute to a group or collective in a positive way, and experience positive self-actualization (not to mention keep your privilege as well).

When you consistently show up a few minutes late to work and your boss doesn't say anything, that's privilege. When you're treated as a family member when a guest in another person's home, that's privilege. When you experience favor in certain social groups, that's privilege.

Being able to experience privilege is a human need, knowing what your privileges are is a blessing. Someone or several people have a vested interest in you. On the other side of you being granted rights by another person or group is their intentions for giving you those rights in the first place. When you're given privilege, it comes on the back of the hopes and expectations of the privilege giver(s).

People allow you to walk in your privilege because of the meaning behind it and what it represents. It's a gesture that implies that if you can experience "XYZ" rights in "QRS" circumstances, then maybe overtly or covertly, some good comes from it. This matters because in the context of a civilization or people choosing to live together for the betterment of all parties involved, there must be a sense of equality. Egalitarianism is a first world problem. It's either a boutique battlefield, or in the event of an egregious violation, a cause for uproar, that could lead to an untenable situation and or the destabilization of a civilization or group. Privilege is an ever-present happy medium in a hierarchical civil system between tyranny and decentralization of government.

Not particularly as a political movement but as a unique experience you can leverage to acquire status and other valuable resources. It serves a similar purpose to egalitarianism on a relatively micro level. That's why you want to manage your privilege well, so that you can maintain and increase your resources. Privileges can also reinforce a person's beliefs in or about a person, place, or thing.

Not everyone is able or will be able to do what you are. Your privileges can be used as building blocks towards your success. Another interesting thing about privilege in law is that it can be transferable. The privilege that I have today is piggy backing off the privilege of those who have gone before me. The same is true for you too. Privilege is not some deep convoluted concept, it's someone or a group seeing something in you or an institution and investing in that something.

White privilege, class privilege, religious privilege, male privilege, female privilege, and the like, are all assumptions. They aren't real. The interesting thing about things that matter is, in some cases the only reason something is real is because it's made real. There can be no inherent truth or rationale to something, but when it's the only message given and heard it can be made manifest. The members of the groups mentioned, and those not, may have certain privileges, but again, a privilege is given.

Politics concerns itself with the governance of people and citizens. For a civilization to exist there must be some form of governance so that people can relate with one another peacefully. In an agriculture-based civilization the government tends to be based on hierarchy. Those at the top and or closer to the top make the rules. The way the people at the top and in charge remain so, is through the levers of politics. The main way this is done is at the expense of those lower on the hierarchy, which is anti-egalitarian in nature and presentation.

At this point there are a whole host of things happening at once. I'll start with you, the individual. Every human being whoever was, is, or will be, needs to become self-actualized. Self-actualization is the experience of you reaching your fullest potential. There are various theories of self-actualization and most psychologists and psychiatrists suggest that it is something everyone can experience. Because self-actualization is a human need you will experience it one way or another, either positively or negatively. Positive self-actualization is behaving more humanly depicted in behaviors and experiences such as, adaptability, spontaneity, a sense of purpose, creativity, and transcendent or flow state experiences. Negative self-actualization is corruption and maladaptivity. When you are denied your humanity, you are primed to act animalistically. Not being able to experience your inalienable rights can be a birthplace for corruption and maladaptiveness.

Because you are inhibited in your ability to experience the fullness of yourself, the way you will likely be intuitively inclined to resolve that dissonance is to behave in a way that is beneath you. Doing things based on carnality, greed, from a place of insecurity, and or to hurt others. The rationale being that if you can't experience the fullness of yourself in a developmentally and experientially for the benefit of others and personal purpose affirming way, you will do things to experience the fullness of yourself in ways that will affirm and perpetuate tyranny in your favor, at the expense of those around you. That type of behavior causes you to live a less satisfying life even if it's a more materially rich one (maybe). And ultimately people who live like that are part of the problem as it relates to not proliferating positivity, enabling themselves or others to innovate and create positive and meaningful contributions, and ensuring the longevity of the human race.

In addition to that, another human need is the right to be treated fairly. Morality and convictions matter. Anyone who tells you to capitulate on your morals is maladaptive and or is trying to corrupt you.

Privilege is disseminated by institutions and various other societal structures and organizations. Some privileges have explicit or implicit approval from a state. A citizenry also contributes to the proliferation of certain privileges for certain people part of said citizenry. Without top down and or bottom up buy in, there is no privilege. Without a mechanism for egalitarianism, agriculture-based civilizations tend to become untenable for those at the bottom of the hierarchy. As part of a hierarchical structure, to satisfy human needs, there must be some kind of privilege available for everyone. The most obvious way privilege presents itself in this way (being available to all) in a hierarchy is within the context of status. At a high-level, status comes with privilege. The good news is status in a hierarchy is decentralized. Wherever you fall in a relative hierarchy, there is some privilege available to you.

Positive self-actualization is cultivated when you can objectively contribute to a group. When you can contribute to a group, that represents individuality from the perspective of self-sustainability, and it reinforces group cohesion from the perspective of your contributions being of value. Self-actualization (positive or negative) from an ecological perspective is how you acquire status in a hierarchy. You demonstrate what you are competent and skilled at and use that knowledge and ability to amass resources and privileges for yourself.

This is where power comes in. The main focus of power

is to maintain what you have. Hierarchies isolate power, making it difficult for the powerful to have things taken from them. Privilege is granted. Within the context of a hierarchy, you don't want to lose what makes you powerful or reinforces your status. Politics is power's best friend. In ways they are derivatives of one another. They both have the aspect of redundancy. Both words share their respective meaning and implication etymologically and or functionally. Power is about movement. Privilege is akin to power, but they differ in experience. Privilege is a tool you can use to acquire resources; power is how you keep those resources. The equation for power in physics is, power equals force multiplied by velocity. Force is acceleration multiplied by time. The equation for acceleration is velocity divided by time. The equation for velocity is displacement divided by time. And the equation for time is distance divided by speed. Speed is distance divided by time. And distance is time divided by speed. Power is redundant, not additive.

Just like the etymology of politics, which is Greek and means the affairs of cities, means what it is about in terms of governance, people, and civilization, power is just as redundant in terms of what is required. Power is your ability to move something quickly in any direction, quickly, and in any direction. As you use your God given gifts, abilities, and talents, to leverage your place in society to gain more privilege for yourself to fulfill multiple physiological needs, you retain your position and resources by displaying power, moving things quickly in any direction, quickly, and in any direction. The main way people do this is through the lens of politics. Humility matters because politics at any level and in any scenario is about serving others. The people who enable your privilege and affirm your status can choose to stop. When people stop buying into a construct it becomes less real.

When you extrapolate this, if people with various privileges don't steward those privileges well, they contribute to the downfall of themselves and at least the people in their sphere of influence, if not the greater group or civilization. No matter how much you have, generosity, fairness, morals, and treating people with dignity always matters.

The more privileges you have presumably the more status you have in a relative hierarchy. The more status you have the better you feel about yourself. The better you feel about yourself the more inclined you are to self-actualize in a positive way. The reverse is the case with the less status you have relative to a hierarchy. Your need to reach your fullest potential is predicated on your ability to do so. When you can't reach your fullest potential or are hindered in some way in doing so, objectively that means there is an infringement on your human right from nature to have the right to access equal opportunities. This is where people can begin to engage in group destroying behaviors because the group isn't helping them become self-actualized in a positive way, and as human beings those people need and will become self-actualized one way or another, good or bad, regardless of cost, because it's a biological need.

On top of your need for self-actualization and your need to experience equality, you also have neurotransmitters, specifically serotonin, that affirm these inclinations in you. Serotonin is a naturally occurring chemical in your brain that lends itself to you feeling confident, having high self-esteem, and feeling a sense of purpose. One of the contributing factors to your serotonin levels is your perception of your status in society. The higher regard you see yourself in relative to your status in a hierarchy, the more serotonin transmits through your brain, therefore the more positively you'll behave (objectively not necessarily conclusively. You can have a high self-image and still engage in maladaptive behaviors). If you hold yourself in low regard relative to your status in society specifically not exclusively, the less serotonin will transmit in your brain, contributing to an increased chance of you potentially engaging in more maladaptive behaviors. You can't escape biology, and privilege, status, and power all have biological implications that are amplified in agriculture-based hierarchical societies. Hierarchies are as old as time and are found everywhere in ecology. They are the best way to survive but not necessarily the best way to govern/be governed.

All of this reinforces the need to understand privilege because it's a critical part of human existence and the gateway through which you can experience your fullest potential. That said, the main way privilege is misused is with respect to power. Because of the zero-sum game nature of hierarchies, people can be misled into believing that inequalities exist because of power imbalances. If someone is more powerful than you it's because they can move things quickly in different directions, quickly, and in different directions, better than you can. Power doesn't mean more stuff; it means more influence. What tends to happen within the context of this misunderstanding is that people may try to exert power to gain more status and privilege. The problem is you can't move what you don't have. The non-physics definition of power is the ability to do something especially or particularly as a matter of fact. Ability comes from ableness and ableness in this context comes from resources. Resources are self-perpetuating, the more you have the more you can get. When you try to exert power to acquire things instead of leveraging what you already have, your acumen, and privilege, you could end up in an adversarial position. Accumulating things for yourself isn't a bad thing. Leading with oppression or tyranny to do so however, disenchants people to your cause.

Instead of valuing privilege that may come naturally to that person or group and applying themselves to develop within that space of possibilities, they will demand and demonstrate for what they want, right or wrong. It would be misguided for me to suggest that there is never a place for demonstration or radical action, power concedes nothing without a demand. What I am referring to boils down to stylization. It's the accumulation of your positive self-actualization, your innate inclination for egalitarianism and other biological factors, a sense of humility, your comprehension of your privileges, and your ability to positively contribute to a collective in a material way, that influences the decisions you make regarding how you go about attaining and maintaining resources for yourself; something that is a human need.

Everyone has privilege. People need to get over the fact that their privilege isn't necessarily the same as someone else's. Stop trying to impose upon other people. Try to win hearts and minds sure, but killing your fellow citizen in the process, literally or metaphorically, is a form of self-harm. The objectification and demonization of the perceived privilege of various people and groups in a society is a means of control.

When the have nots are too busy fighting with each other, the haves can sleep good at night knowing that the people who enable them by affirming their privilege, are in such disarray that they will never find the wherewithal in themselves, to overcome their differences long enough to realize who put them against each other in the first place. Regardless of societal influences and institutions, you are just as privileged as your neighbor. When you get out of your national politics and consider your own life and personal ecology, there are things you are allowed to do, privileges given that are unique to you. The same goes for some other person in their own relative ecology.

Sometimes we zoom out too much in life. And while that is the nature of societal living what can also happen when you zoom out too much is you lose detail and nuance. Before you are part of a larger community, you are part of a local community in your home, on your block, and in your neighborhood. There are no differences between people besides the ones we delineate or have delineated for us and then buy into.

Humility matters in general and with respect to privilege because, freedom is how we feel most alive. Enjoying life is better than fearing death. At your core you know this. This is a higher-level need concern because most people have agreed or at least consented to the reality of forgoing some freedom to experience longevity. In the nooks and crannies of all that, however, are opportunities for you to go back to the state of nature from an additive perspective. You will have the opportunity to be a better person when you have access to certain rights and privileges. Humility in that experience will open doors for similar experiences. This is how you can get the most out of life.

CHAPTER 7

How to Have and Keep a Goal

Having a goal, a dream, or a vision of growth for your life can be difficult. Are you familiar with burnout? Burnout is a feeling of being physically, emotionally, and mentally exhausted. You have no will to continue. This happens when you allow yourself to get overwhelmed by the various environmental stimuli in your life.

Sometimes, you can get fatigued in your spirit as well. Maybe you were hoping for something good to happen, and that good never happened. Maybe you are working to start/grow a business, but no matter how much resources you put into it, that business is struggling with getting off the ground.

Is it possible that there is some deep desire you started pursuing, but life got in the way and took you off course?

What do you do when what you have is not representative of what you want? How can you keep going when the world is telling you to stop or even worse, turn around?

As humans, we get tired. We need sleep, we need rest. But sometimes you can also get tired in your circumstances. An expectation is a hope for an anticipated future. To have an expectation implies that you are believing for something to manifest in your life.

Burnout/fatigue can happen when you are in a constant state of hoping, wishing, and taking actionable steps towards your goals, but nothing seems to be happening. If you have found or currently find yourself in this position, here are a few ways to combat "expectation burnout:"

The Law of Diminishing Returns

One thing for you to understand is that you may be experiencing the side effects of what is called the Law of Diminishing Returns. This universal law says that as you grow in your knowledge/skill for something, the rate at which you recognize continued growth in that subject matter starts to diminish. As you build on existing knowledge what's left to learn becomes more nuanced and subsequently less noticeable (and notably more experiential and or circumstantial).

This tends to happen because the information that you learn at the beginning stages of something is usually the newest in terms of concept, and the most pertinent in terms of execution.

By the time you know the essentials of something, the

growth margins become a lot smaller. The bulk of learning something is usually front loaded. At the point of relative peak on a learning curve, things start to drastically level out.

Sometimes you must shift your mindset. You may think you're not growing in an area of your life when in reality, that growth has just become more subtle and tempered. Eventually all growth and progress become less about the rate at which you are growing, and more about the quality of growth that is taking place. If you find yourself in a place of hopelessness, in a funk, and or unsure on how to get out, get more detailed about what you do.

This has happened in my life. At one point I noticed that my growth in various areas of my life was becoming stagnant. I knew I had things to accomplish, but I felt like doing those things alone was not sufficient if I wanted to hit my goals. The other issue was, I felt as though I was doing all that I could and that there was nothing for me to improve on.

What I realized was, the skills that I had available to me at that time were in fact sufficient, but I was not using them sufficiently.

Sometimes you must get granular with your progress. How can you improve on the action behind the action? This is where consistent growth lives because you are actively looking for improvement.

Be Detail Oriented

The "small" consistent actions you make today, will have a significant long-term payoff. The notion behind this is that by doing something repetitiously, you are growing because you are building on your progress.

Repetition is the mother of learning, and a key

component of success. When you are always learning something new that is taking you closer to your goals, you are being successful.

The problem with this is that it can be monotonous. The way in which you combat that, is by making the monotony important. It's that extra level of care for the small things that will make you better at your craft. Become familiar with the intricacies of a thing. Learn to incorporate that aspect of those things prominently in your work.

Part of a growth mindset is being able to find value in the little things. If you are diligent in the small things, you will be confident and capable of handling the bigger things.

It's Okay to Take a Step Back

What is more important: the goal, or when you accomplish said goal? In most cases one would probably say that taking longer to achieve what they want is better than, failing at trying to do it at a faster pace.

You do not have to be a super person!

If you are feeling fatigued/overwhelmed, it is okay to take a personal day. Refresh and collect your thoughts. Allow yourself to find new muses, and sources of inspiration. You are taking part in the creative process when you do this.

Some of my best ideas come to me while I am disconnecting from my aspirational pursuits and connecting with loved ones. This is because new experiences invite us to explore and uncover different paradigms. Having revelation, the introduction of new knowledge into your life, is also part of the creative process.

If you don't give yourself time to decompress, your mental capacity will become foggy. Take a step back and allow for new ideas to naturally flow. You never know when the next idea will be the right idea, so stay in position to receive; but also extend to yourself the grace of not having to commoditize everything that presents itself to you.

Reevaluate the Size of your Dream

How big is your dream? How lofty are your goals? One good way to combat expectation fatigue is to realign yourself with your goals. Why are you doing what you are doing in the first place?

Sometimes you can stand in the way of your own growth simply by being out of alignment with what you want to accomplish. Big goals come equipped with a rutter. If you find that you are having a hard time excelling in your life, maybe now is a good time to reconsider what you are actually after. It's said that expectations are the killer of joy. That doesn't mean you can't or shouldn't have them. It does mean, however, that maybe you should balance your expectations with some relative objectivity. All things that become real and last in your life come from work. You shouldn't/can't expect what you didn't put the quality and quantity of work necessary, in for. Don't expect to be the greatest if you don't or didn't do what the greatest do and did. But also, don't let that discourage you, because you can still find as much success as you want relative to your life and blaze a new trail.

I know I tend to not give it my best for something that I don't want. And there are things that I've wanted that I've had to reconsider, because for reason or another, I never committed the work necessary to experience a realistic expectation at a high level in that area of life. Being out of alignment with your goals could mean that you are going after something of diminished value. Is what you want still what you want, and are you actually pursuing it, or did you get off track somewhere along the way?

This has happened to me several times before, where I was doing something that I thought I should be doing; but eventually, I would burnout, and run out of energy. After taking time to reevaluate what I was doing, I would find that what I was doing and what I thought would help me progress, was just me standing in my own way. I wasn't taking actions that reflected what my main goals were.

Taking time to reconsider your dreams also helps you to discover the scale and scope of that dream. A good dream and aspiration have space for others. Who is included in your plans? You can also thwart yourself by not having a large enough goal. The value in having a big goal is that there is room to grow within that goal.

A small goal can be limiting because of its feasibility. If you identify that you want to do something, and that something that you want doesn't push you to overcome yourself in some way, you really didn't do anything worth doing. Having an expectation is about giving yourself something to be ambitious about.

You demonstrate that you have hope through the work that you are willing to commit to your goals. If you believe that you want something to come to pass, you must work for it. It's in the work that things get accomplished. And it's the accomplishing of things that makes other things manifest and materialize. A dream without a plan is just a wish. Only wishing for things is not a particularly wise way to live your life.

If you are getting tired in doing what needs to be done for you to excel and achieve your goals, consider the fact that, you are closer to your dream than you even realize. Don't give up! But also give yourself time to rest and reevaluate.

Expectations are great to have but are even better when they are working in your favor. Burnout and fatigue can happen to anyone, consider it a worthy opponent and not an obstacle. You don't have to go through life tripping over yourself. Align yourself with your goals and dreams by having ones that while are achievable, challenge you to go above and beyond; and commit to them.

CHAPTER 8

Why it's Important to Be Resilient

Being resilient means being elastic. Its toughness. You bend but you don't break. My grandmother would say, "you have to be able to take a licking and keep on ticking." It's emotional strength and conviction. Its grit. It's a decided belief that you cannot and will not fail.

You need to be resilient because one of the inevitabilities of life is coming up against opposition. You will have challenges. As long as you are alive something somewhere that is unfavorable will rear its ugly head. What are you going to do when your problems come for you?

It's important that I talk about this because while I focus on being healthy and having the right mindset mostly, life can sometimes be unforgiving. What do you do when things are not going in your direction?

I can be competitive. It's not really a problem for me as much as it can be an issue for those around me. That being said, I think it's okay to say that having a competitive mindset has contributed to my ability to survive and navigate life. I've had no other option but to be resilient. Failure is not a permanent condition; and I would rather not use my labeling power for negativity.

The Bible says that the first job God gave Adam was to name all the animals. You have the power to dictate to and or label things in your life. Who do you call you? What do you label yourself as? I have never found it comforting identifying as a failure.

Resilience is having passion and perseverance. You must be willing to persevere for what you're passionate (have a strong emotion) about. Typically, people have passion, but they do not have perseverance. Passion is what gets you started, but perseverance is what keeps you going.

You must learn to endure. This comes from having resolve. Anyone who does not stand for anything will fall for everything. Where is your proverbial line in the sand? What is the thing that you are unwilling to capitulate on?

Why do you do what you do? Who you are is more important than what you do and what you do should be informed by who you are.

Does who you are dictate to what you do? Resilient people label their circumstances rather than giving into the reverse. This can be aligned with having a growth mindset. I may have failed at something, but I am not a failure. Do you believe that about yourself? What do you do in the face of opposition?

These are things that we have to develop as individuals. What has worked for me may not work for you; There are vast and unique ways to build resolve. However, one thing that is required is you must at the very least, hold yourself in high regard.

Are you accountable, and do you have follow through power? Being able to follow through-do what you said you would do-as often as possible is something that is important. One sure way to build resilience in yourself is to commit to yourself, this especially includes what you say.

You are not tethered to your reality. What you see is not all that is. That is why the most important person that can speak life into your situation is you. Don't look for from others what you aren't willing to do for yourself.

CHAPTER 9

What to do When You are Frustrated

What do you do when you have done everything you can? It's not your fault when life decides to start presenting itself as working against you; but it is your fault if *you* decide to start working against it.

Frustration happens when you are in total alignment and yet and still there is no breakthrough. It is a rather pragmatic issue. If you are doing everything within your power and things are still not working in your favor, the first thing anyone would tend to do is dissect what the issue is.

Sometimes however, even after dissecting the issue and trying to understand why things aren't working out, you can still struggle to find a reason. Have you ever tried putting something together and you do not have all the materials you need, but you do not find out until halfway through the build?

When you're frustrated, building on progress can be one of the most difficult things you could do.

Why would anyone keep working at something that is obviously not working/producing anything? There is no answer aside from hope and passion.

If you genuinely want something you must want every aspect of that thing. That means the ups and the downs, the valleys, and the mountains. So, what should you do when you don't know what to do? Keep doing what you are doing. I know, it can be a tough pill to swallow, and not the answer that I would necessarily want to hear, but once again this is a pragmatic issue.

The first thing to address is your perception of the situation. What is the source of your frustration? After Identifying the what, then you must uncover the why. After the why is revealed the next thing to do is to discover the how, how can you mitigate your frustration? The following are ways you can do just that:

Look for Help Outside of Yourself

What happens is, the root of your frustration more often than not is a clear and concise issue without a clear and concise resolution. What this means is, you may not be able to solve this problem on your own. In this type of circumstance, all you can do is all that you can do.

Frustration is a practical problem that requires an outside intervention. Not only can we not do life by ourselves, but we also can't solve all our problems exclusively either. Every once in a while, everyone needs some help.

With others, you can discuss your thoughts, receive new perspectives, and come to new resolutions. Coaches, mentors, and accountability partners are great in times like these. Sometimes in moments of frustration, what can be really helpful is taking a moment to vent.

Do not neglect your right to "complain." I put "complain" in quotations because a moment of emotional release should not devolve into a bash session. You are not discontent in your circumstance(s); you are distressed by it (them). Sometimes your will to grow is larger than your capacity. You are ready to climb the mountain, but you cannot find where the trail starts.

It's Okay to be Angry

In these moments it is important to express your anger. Find a safe space whether that be in a journal, with a loved one, a blog, podcast, an open lot (to yell and scream) or otherwise; and release how you feel. Finding different ways to release my frustrations is how I got started on my entrepreneurial path.

Getting your feelings off your chest is important for a myriad of reasons. When you harbor anger, you allow resentment to grow. Expressing your negative emotions allows you to be free in your feelings. At the end of the day, the last thing you should want is to feel as though you are not in control of yourself.

Letting go of your negative emotions will also help you problem solve better. I personally can't think straight when my mind is cluttered. When you emote your gripes, you allow yourself to free up some of your mental capacity so that you can begin to process things more logically.

Ask for What You Want

Don't be afraid to ask for what you want. The good thing about being frustrated about something is that in most cases, you know what you want/need to relieve you of your discomfort. Don't be afraid to ask for it. Part of activating the law of attraction in your life is asking for what you desire.

If you find yourself frustrated do not hesitate to ask God/the universe for relief. The Universe is conspiring for you not against you. Feeling frustrated is part of the growing process.

The good news is, God wants to see you grow. If you are living in alignment yet find yourself in a place of frustration, express those feelings. Do not deviate from your plans and remember that life is here to shape you, not break you.

You are a spiritual being having a physical experience. You can have anything you believe you are worthy of receiving. Tap into your "why power" and push forward. The frustration will pass, and when it does, the breakthrough on the other side will be too marvelous to comprehend!

CHAPTER 10

Believing is a Choice

You generate your belief through your behavior. You show that you believe something while simultaneously strengthening that belief "muscle." The more you demonstrate your belief the more that belief codifies within you. What you think translates into what you do, which affirms what you believe. This looks like for example someone thinking they can't get ahead, acting in ways that don't promote promotion, and then as a result, accepting what they are experiencing. Or a person who speaks highly of themself, is goal oriented, and takes the necessary steps to advance their agenda and experience their desired results. In either scenario it's self-fulfilling prophecy.

When you accept something, you are consenting to receive. What are you willing to allow to happen to you? That's choice. Every choice you make you are giving permission for something to happen to, for, around, or in you. Choices are a byproduct of knowledge. Knowledge is not the only contributor to choice but action on a choice starts as a thought. If you can think better, you can live better.

Compartmentalization can help with thinking better and this is not exclusively a quantity of knowledge thing. It's not about how much you know; it's about how well you deploy what you know. This incorporates a multitude of things, not the least of which being wisdom. Living better is fundamentally a quality-of-life experience. People can tend to conflate quality-of-life with other things. Quality-of-life doesn't have to be the fruits of your contributions to capitalism.

Just because you can acquire more things doesn't mean you'll be happy. And even happiness is a red herring or at least deceptive, because happiness is a feeling not a state of being. You can be happy and broke. Happy and in a hospital or happy while on a rocket ship to the moon. Happiness has nothing to do with your condition. Living better implies thriving over surviving. And thriving as a bare-bones interpretation implies having at least enough. There is a fine line between enough and greed.

This is where ideology enters the chat. What do you objectively think about the world you live in? Once you understand your ideology and how that influences your behaviors, then you can start to make changes in your belief system and ultimately in your life. It's a serious place to arrive at. Accepting to be responsible for your actions can be difficult.

CHAPTER 11

God In The Struggle

The hardest thing to accomplish is inner peace. The absurdity of life is everlasting. Jesus tells us that in this world we will struggle and or have trials but that he has overcome those things. How does one overcome life's barrage of trials? One of the interesting things about Jesus is that he is fully divine and fully human. During his time on earth, he got to experience [with other humans] the human condition. A common mode of transportation back then was boat travel. The gospels account at least two times where the winds of life within the context of a body of water created cognitive dissonance for Jesus' disciples.

In the face of wind, Peter sunk (Matthew 14:22-33). And in the face of wind, the disciples feared for their lives (Mark 4:35-41). Seeing wind on the water is significant because of the clarity of the vestige it provides. Wind over water still creates waves. Your perception of wind over land could get distorted by other contributing factors to the storm, mainly particles and debris. Wind over water has such a unique simplicity to it that it's one of the ways God first introduces himself in Genesis chapter 1 of the Bible.

The significance of bringing up winds in this context is to display that regardless of whether it be literal or metaphorical, the winds of life are commonplace. Extrapolate the aforementioned examples within the context of your own life and uncover for yourself how many times you can identify the winds of life: struggles, hardships, difficult situations to navigate, infirmity, trials, and the like. The winds of life are not man made. There is a teleological nature to them.

In the Garden of Eden God puts the Tree of the Knowledge of Good and Evil some theologians may suggest, right in the middle of the garden. The tree literally represents death (Genesis 2:17). Juxtaposed to the literal, is the philosophical representation of the ability for Adam and Eve to acquire knowledge. Adam and Eve saw in the tree something that they didn't have and maybe didn't really want, but that nonetheless created dissonance and struggle in a place that is considered to be utopian in nature.

Why would God put struggle in a perfect place and only allow his presence to be made manifest in the winds (Genesis 3:8)? Imagine every day you go to work trying to do the right thing, but on your way coming and going you have to pass this object of ridicule, which exists at least in some degree to remind you of the fact that you are not smart and are potentially incompetent. This is struggle, this is trial, this is absurdity. At face value it doesn't make any sense why trials may exist even in heavenly places.

Philosophers reveal to us that there is no meaning to the things that we endure in life other than to endure them. If absurdity is built into life's equation, then the challenge for you and arguably one of the highest calls for a person, is to therefore quell the gesticulations of their inner man. You must learn to quiet your inner voice. You must have the courage of your convictions to silence your worries. This doesn't mean not acknowledging your worries, it means being determined, unwavering, and resolute in that you are stronger than any negative experiences you may go through.

You have nothing to fear but fear itself. Fear is what causes you to make premature decisions. Fear can also cause you to not make any decision at all. Embrace what you are afraid of. This means embracing death. Everyone dies. Your odds of dying are higher than not dying. If you had to bet on dying or living forever, you're probably better off betting on the former. Death is the next phase of life for a plurality of people. Once you're not afraid to die for what you believe then you can go against absurdity.

Another thing to note about death is that the possibility of death is all around you. Besides your mortality, you can also experience a social death. A social death is a death blow to your identity. Losing a job, making a fool of yourself around other people, the fallout from making a poor decision, and more are example of a social death. Whether moral or social, your character needs to be fortified enough to withstand the possibility of whatever, in whatever scenario, to rise above the anxiety that may come with the ever-changing tides of life.

You don't have to live your life in a maddening way. If what you are doing is driving you crazy, you don't need to keep doing it. This is the lie of profit driven marketplaces. People in western civilizations, specifically not exclusively, are often sold the lie that if they trade their time for monetary notes it will result in a sense of peace and security. If you work your bills will be paid, you'll have healthcare (in America), and you'll have a house. If you don't work, that's unfortunate to say the least. Who's not considered are the people who are somewhere in the middle who can't afford to not work but are also not afforded meaningful work. And from personal experience, if your work asks you to submit to it, pledge your allegiance to it, and or compromise on your convictions for it, and that's something you don't want to or can't do for various reasons, then you shouldn't do that work/work for that employer.

The good news is there is another way. You can go against the status quo. You can forge your own path. Living that way comes with its own challenges and risks, but the risk of life is risk. To be alive (born and drawing breath) is risk, and to live (do something with yourself) is risk. When you've come to the end of yourself and aren't afraid of dying, the concern isn't the risk itself, it's the opportunity for reward. What's a better situation for you, struggling and going nowhere, or struggling and getting somewhere?

Contemporary economic systems long to make you complacent in your ownershiplessness. You may not have or own any longevity or generational wealth, but at least you're anesthetized with materialism and the byproduct of profit you produce but don't retain a lion's share of. That's not a normal pattern of living outside of a corrupt system.

Now imagine that you live a life where you have nothing to lose and everything to live for. The risk of that life pales in comparison to the risk of being too afraid to pursue it. This is where God resides in the struggle. You encounter God at this part of the struggle because it's here where you realize that he is the only thing worth living for; less you become a nihilist. When you're on a journey for your life, the accoutrements of your life are less influential. Your nouns don't matter. People, places, and things are nice, but they are all fleeting. If you're not willing to let those things go at any moment they will be taken from you, ultimately via death, theirs, or yours. Nouns are part of the journey, not the pinnacle.

This is also a great point to process any aspect of a slave mentality that you may have. A slave mentality is a mindset that rationalizes struggles as inevitabilities as opposed to opportunities to rise to the occasion. Just because struggles are prolific doesn't mean you have to give yours virtues. The other aspect of struggle is context. As has been shown struggle is universal, but what are the mitigating and contributing factors of a specific struggle? Not every struggle is wholly a condition of your existence. There are things you can do something about in almost any circumstance. And the same goes for the things that you can't do anything about. Take control of your own destiny by doing something about the things that you can do something about, and not concerning yourself about those things which you can't.

This is one of the ways God intended for us to grow in life. Ignore the proverbial Tree of the Knowledge of Good and Evil in your life. Walk by faith. Absurdity is teleological in nature. All things work together for your good when you love God and are following his call and will for your life. Your proverbial Tree of the Knowledge of Good and Evil relative to any context may not have anything to do with work or self-concept, but nevertheless it's a test of your self- fortitude. True humanity is rising to the challenge of life. God is alive, and he is in your struggle. He always will and has no problem coming to you, but for you to grow in depth and effectiveness he wants you to come to him.

CHAPTER 12

Justice

Justice is divine in nature. Your ability to create stems from the supreme creator. Justice is a product of divine creativity. Your morals contribute to the degree at which you shine with the reflection of God. Justice is just doing, doing justly towards your fellow human(s) and treating them according to their imbued God given dignity.

This is the highest hope one can aspire to next to the return of Jesus Christ himself, who is the embodiment of justice. Say what you want about hope but one thing it does well is contribute to perseverance. The active anticipation of worldwide righteousness is the greatest of life's calls.

In the face of the madness and chaos of life the courageous thing to do is to believe that justice, good, righteousness, and wholesomeness exists and will make itself made manifest. This looks like an obliteration of things that are immoral. Chaos can run rampant because chaos is immediate. Think of a shock to a system. In the immediate there may be a sharp response. Chaos is something that ensues quickly and settles slowly.

Chaos is the context of justice. Chaos itself is not the thing that is chaotic. Chaos has a defined end. What makes chaos chaotic (confusing and or disorderly) is the method taken to arrive to said end. The end cannot justify the means in a just world, otherwise people can justify any of their actions and claim that what they are doing is for some greater good. Chaos happens quickly through confusion and disorder, but those things have a predictable and correct conclusion. Time extrapolates chaos by allowing it to diverge. Chaos is the domino effect of one thing impacting another impacting something else.

What this means for justice is that it either comes quickly, or over time, but usually not in the immediate (promptly after a chaos catalyst is triggered) or the interim (in the middle of chaos proliferating). Justice tends to let chaos have its moment before intervening. Justice is reactionary in nature; a problem needs to be solved because something created that problem initially. Righteousness is the behavior that justice informs and is affirmed by. When you live righteously you perpetuate doing the just or morally appropriate thing. This kind of behavior is supremely valuable in an unjust and chaotic world. Lower case "j" justice is a proliferation of right doing in the pursuit of equality among people and or people groups. Capital "j" justice is the final end to the chaos.

In philosophy this is where the meaning of life comes from, in pursuing happiness in the context of the chaotic and disorderly. The Bible says that the ultimate happiness will be when believers are face to face with God and Jesus. That's something to believe and hope for. That's capital "J" Justice.

CHAPTER 13

How to Compartmentalize

With the complexities that life sometimes presents you with it can be hard to find time for a break. Your mind is constantly stimulated and distracted by social media, ads, your personal circumstances, and more. If you are not cognizant of your needs for stability you can run the risk of burnout or sheer mental and physical exhaustion. One way to keep yourself from being overwhelmed by the nouns of [your] life is to learn to compartmentalize.

Compartmentalize means to divide something up into different categories. Think of it like the different rooms of a house, only in this case the house would be your mind, and the different rooms would be the things that you allow yourself to give attention to.

This is an important skill to have on a myriad of levels. It shows you what you consider valuable in your life, it helps with problem solving, it can improve your interpersonal relationships, make you more productive, and help you live in alignment. With this skill, and these techniques, you can improve your quality of life.

Know Your Triggers

What gets you upset? What makes you uncomfortable? Are there things that you are actively concerned about? These questions allude to the circumstances in which your triggers can be made manifest. A mental or emotional trigger is something that elicits a maladaptive response from you. You can tend to respond in this way because a trigger is generally associated with something relatively traumatic in your life.

If you were bullied growing up for example, then you may not take kindly to that behavior or the people engaging in it, if and when it presents itself in your life. Or if another certain kind of behavior is perpetuated around you that you don't like, you may respond viscerally. Triggers can be overcome. The challenge of a trigger, however, is in knowing how to mitigate and regulate your emotions and behaviors around them. Triggers can put you in a survival mode from the perspective of activating your fight or flight response. They stem from a certain place or environment, or they can pop up in a real time situation. Additionally, they can have the attribute of being re-occurring. Your triggers are the first thing you need to identify because they cause distress.

Your goal in trying to progress through your day should be not tripping over any obstacles. This isn't to say that obstacles will not appear, but rather when they do, you want to have the ability to conquer them. Sometimes overcoming a roadblock means going another way, and that's okay too. Part of knowing your triggers is knowing what is and what isn't worth your time, energy, and or other resources.

Prioritize

Are your priorities in order? After handling your trigger(s) the next thing that you should be looking to do is the thing that will progress your day to the next point. Your priorities should be things that matter to you and have a clear and distinct order of importance.

Your priorities reflect what you value, and what you value is put on display by where and how you spend your time. Time of course is your most important commodity. So essentially you should be giving your time to things that matter most in descending order.

Another valuable thing to do is to develop a routine around your priorities. Most of us have a core group of activities that we do consistently throughout the week. Building a regimen around those essential activities helps you to transition through your day smoothly. It also becomes a fail safe for you to be able to revert to the next part of your routine to help you continue through your day.

Be Adaptable

One thing to always keep in the back of your mind is the fact that life happens. Sometimes things will take place that are out of your control. When and if that happens focus on keeping a cool and level head (don't catastrophize or jump to conclusions too soon).

Being able to meet the needs of a moment is a survival skill. You have to be able to identify direction. Do you know where you are going? If you know your purpose, then the way you get there is not as important. Living in alignment is about doing what meets your present need and one of the ways you do that is through being able to adapt to various situations. Being able to address the needs of your life and adapt to them will make you more effective and impactful.

Be Intentional

The idea here is that you want to do things on purpose with purpose. Intentionality is an essence. It's concern about your passion. It's compassion about your plight and the plight of others. It should cause you to want to act in a way that will make a situation better.

The purpose for intentionality is understanding. People don't pay attention to what they don't value. What's important to you? Discovering whether and how you are intentional in a certain activity will reveal what is valuable to you. Once you have learned what matters to you the next step is to do that activity with diligence and excellence. This means among other things being present. You should do what you do with purpose and or for a good reason. The goal of compartmentalization is to help you get through your day while reducing the probability of unhealthy stress.

Don't do things just to do them. You need to have a base level rationale for your actions. Compartmentalization is unhelpful within the context of nebulousness. Ultimately there are only two directions for your life to go in, forward or nowhere; and you must choose between them. Actively choosing not to progress is counter intuitive to the design of life. Everything progresses or ages in some capacity. Your life should be geared towards a progressive direction otherwise you may end up meandering, with nothing to show for yourself or your efforts.

Keep Your Eyes on the Prize

A goal is something you hope for-a reason to get out of bed in the morning. The value in having goals is that they help you direct your life. The Bible says that without vision the people perish. You must be able to see yourself on the proverbial mountain top, driving the new car, with the millions of dollars, furnishing a new home, having a beautiful family, or whatever it is. And it doesn't have to be that deep (existential in nature), sometimes your goal could be to make it back to your bed at the end of the day.

A goal just gives you something to strive for. People do not strive for enough in their life. Or they allow their dreams to die, settling for what they already have. This type of thought process and or behavior is aligned with a slave mentality. You are a spiritual being having a physical experience meaning that your desires would not have been put in you if they were not meant to be fulfilled through you. When you have a big enough goal to aspire to, you can't help but think about it frequently. A true goal/passion will play through your head like a movie on constant rerun. You should be infatuated with the promise on your life (your desires). In doing so you motivate yourself to be better today than you were yesterday.

Compartmentalization is a great skill to develop in your life. It keeps you on track and helps you navigate your world and yourself. The idea behind this skill is that you are hyper focused on what's in front of you. This doesn't mean you become distracted and wishy washy, quite the opposite. When you compartmentalize you become more effective because you choose with intention what you give your attention to. You allow your priorities to inform the narrative of your day. Through identifying and confronting the roadblocks in your life, having your priorities in order, being able to adapt to whatever life may throw at you, doing things on purpose with purpose, and keeping your eyes on the prize; you can develop your own compartmentalization skill.

CHAPTER 14

Why You Struggle with Supporting Yourself

Support starts in the family. A family is the built-in support system of life. That's where your sense of self starts. If support wasn't important nature wouldn't have made it our natural disposition. Support lends itself to your survival in several ways. Having the right support can be the difference maker in the kind of opportunities life presents to you. If you have a good support system you can, for example, get promoted easier, gain traction in various endeavors quicker, walk through doors you may otherwise not have access to, and be protected from things that may be disastrous. If you have no support system, or an ideologically poor one, you might as well be doing life upstream and without a paddle; brace yourself for a bumpy ride and try to make it.

Self-confidence is when you mix self-impression with

your beliefs. You have self-confidence when you believe in what you see in the mirror and when what you see in the mirror has some virtue. The reason you may struggle with having self-confidence (supporting yourself) is because no one ever cultivated anything positively meaningful about you for you to believe in. To support yourself or anything for that matter, there must be something to support. If no one has ever acknowledged meaningful aspects of your humanity in an affirming way (appearance, personality, character, capabilities, or proclivities), it can be difficult for you to know what about yourself you should support.

This leads to you struggling to support yourself because instead of confidence you have doubts and questions, or worse, misguided beliefs. This looks like instead of saying for example, "I am beautiful, I am smart, and I am determined," asking, "am I beautiful, smart, or determined?" Or in the case of a misguided belief, saying that you don't have certain qualities. If the positive and virtuous aspects of you are not properly nurtured over time, it can result in you having a hard time drawing a definitive affirmative conclusion about those aspects of yourself. Support is self- sufficient. If support needs support, then it's not inherently support. You may have a weak internal constitution because it was never properly fortified in you to begin with.

Another issue is that you may not be getting the right kind of support that will enable you to support yourself. If you always have to ask someone for permission before you can make a decision, that's not support. If you had support in that scenario, it would have come with a default level of trust. If someone only affirms the negative in your life it can be difficult to believe [in] the positive. If all your life you've been called ugly or busted, and one day an attractive suitable partner comes around and says you're the most gorgeous thing they've ever seen, you may think they must have seen some real ugly people before you. It can be difficult to believe something today that hasn't been true for you for years.

Additionally, you can also be affirmed or cultivated in an area of your life/aspect of yourself that is straight up not true. Growing up my family and certain mentors in my life said I should try to be a preacher, that I would be good at it, and could earn a decent living. The issue there was, being a preacher wasn't in the cards for me. When someone affirms something in you that isn't true that can lead to confusion and dysfunction as well. People may not engage in this type of activity insidiously or maliciously, though some may. Maybe someone sees something in you that you don't see in yourself. That being said, a quality doesn't necessarily transfer over to a belief system.

I am a Christian, I love God, I went to seminary, and I speak publicly on occasions. I have spoken at churches before and all Christians are called to discipleship, however, none of those things lend themselves to my self-expression beyond personally. My faith influences what I do, as it should, but I have no real preaching aspirations, and preaching isn't a motivating factor for me. In the same way, if someone cultivates something in you that doesn't align with how you see yourself, it won't lend itself to allowing you to support yourself.

That being said also, however, sometimes people may see a gift or talent in you that they are unfamiliar with as it relates to their ability to articulate the concept; so, they will use their schemas to try to make sense of your life for themselves. That's not always helpful or supportive either. And this is where several things can go wrong for you too; because someone else's life or lived experience isn't yours. And though they may think they are being helpful, and again some people may be being deceitful in this manner as well, when people try to put you somewhere you don't belong or fit, it's likely you'll struggle with self-concept and self-actualization.

There was a time when I was down on my luck, and my family kept saying, "don't worry about it, you'll bounce back, you're still young." While those words were nice and I understood and appreciated what they were saying, it didn't resonate with me in a way that cultivated a positive self-impression. Someone would say "you're still young," and all I'd hear is, "you're a failure and will never amount to anything until two days before you die."

Support is crucial but if it's not the right kind of support, or a type of support that will encourage you to support yourself, then it's quintessentially unsupportive. If you've experienced or are currently experiencing something like this, the way you can begin to support yourself is by identifying the areas of your life that you want to be supported in.

No one is perfect. People may try to project their thoughts, feelings, and insecurities onto you. You need to be encouraged and emboldened to say that certain things are not helpful to you, and that you would like [those] things to be done differently.

That's the first step to supporting yourself, speaking up for yourself. You may go through periods and seasons of life where good support is nowhere to be found. In those times it's up to you to identify and strengthen your own redeeming qualities. You need to know what makes you special. You also need to know what makes you feel special. Having a sober awareness of your qualities will make it easier for you to support you because you'll know you.

Don't set yourself up for failure by thinking that you

can't find support or create your own support group. You may have to adjust your understanding of support. Everyone may not be able to help you in every situation, but surely someone can help you in a particular situation. Also, just because people are around doesn't mean they are supportive. Some people give off non playable character energy. Their purpose in your life is presence not necessarily function. Be willing and unashamed to advocate for yourself in all areas of your life. When you have little to no support the best thing to do is build your own support apparatus, and that starts with you developing and having support for yourself (you supporting you).

CHAPTER 15

Dealing with Other People's Insecurities

In psychology there is a human behavior identified as projection. Projection is when a person, instead of admitting to and owning their thoughts, feelings, emotions, behaviors, and beliefs, blames or abdicates that responsibility to some other noun. For example, let's say you wear your hair a certain way, and someone you know almost always has some type of negative reaction to your hairstyle. On top of being a hater, that person may also be projecting their internal feelings onto you because you're confident and or comfortable enough to be yourself in a way that they are not.

When they see you, they see either what they want to be, or what they know they can't be. That can stir up some type of internal conflict in that person that they don't have the wherewithal to embrace and or handle themselves, so they project those feelings onto you. Not all criticism comes from a good place. You may be living your life right now based off something someone with less creativity and ability said to you because they projected those feelings onto you; and you listened because you trust that person. Hurt people hurt people, that includes your people too.

The road to hell is paved by good intentions. How many times does someone who is "just looking out for you" or "has your best interest at heart," say or do something that is either opposite those sentiments, or is out of alignment with what you want and value in your life? These types of people are not honest dealers. They hate you because they ain't you. They see in you what they wish they had in themselves. Or maybe they have it, but they haven't cultivated it the way you have. Projection or projecting is considered a defense mechanism.

A defense mechanism is an identity-based behavior that is in place by someone's consciousness to protect them from things that may induce stress, anxiety, and or a fight or flight response. There are various types of defense mechanisms, and all people have them, the difference is not everyone's defense mechanism is designed to hurt someone else. When someone projects onto someone else, there can be unforeseen fallout on the part of the person being projected onto.

If you at first believe you can accomplish anything you put your mind to, but then someone comes along and says that you can't, if you trust and believe that person or sentiment, you could end up spinning your wheels. You'll struggle with cognitive dissonance in a way that frankly you should have never been initially exposed to.

My relationship with this topic is very personal, and sometimes I feel as though I talk about this subject a bit too often on my website (lifewithken.com). The people who projected onto me the most negatively were my family and friends. And there is a whole host of problems when your enemy has you on speed dial. I can't help that certain people in my life are so insecure that they rather tear themselves down through me, instead of encouraging me to become something that might benefit all of us as a whole. The unfortunate part is that as a person with some dignity and self-respect, fundamentally I can't allow that type of behavior to persist around me.

There are people who are relatively relationally close to me, that will never read this book, will only visit my website to hate, and or will try to cast spells and conduct some type of witchcraft against me, all because they are untalented losers too afraid to accept their shortcomings and do something about them. That is not my fault nor is it my plight. The same is the case for you. When someone presents themselves as insecure whether it be through a defense mechanism like projection, or some other means, it's not your job to pacify them or suffer their maladaptive behavior to make them feel better.

Don't worry about what someone said you couldn't do. I bet that if they said you couldn't do it, they probably aren't doing it themselves. They are mad that you have the audacity to live by your convictions. The truth is they may be mad that you have convictions at all. They're haters. A hater or opposition is someone who is against you and or your efforts. They won't come out of their face and say it all the time, but they harbor that feeling or those feelings inside of themselves. People will hate for a multitude of reasons, but that shouldn't be your concern, less you become a hater yourself.

The best thing you can do in the face of opposition or another person's insecurities is get away. Don't let someone else's emotional whirlwinds cause damage in your life. Who cares what their intentions are if their behaviors are not aligned with your desires. Your desires are divinely inspired. Certain people may not want you to be successful, but God does. They may not care or want you to finish school, but God wants you to finish school. Certain people may not care or want you to start a family, but God wants you to have a family. Whatever your aspirations are, they wouldn't be in you if God didn't want them to be fulfilled through you.

Don't give people power they don't have. That's exactly what they want. Someone who is incapable of self- actualizing themselves meaningfully and virtuously will try to hinder your growth as much as they can and at every step of the way. Their shortcomings aren't your problem, don't let them try to make them so. Now not all criticism is insecurity or hate, and detraction can be good in that it keeps you honest. That being said, be critical of the source. Who is saying something to you and what is that person's track record? Are they saying something that is in alignment with your beliefs (not necessarily affirming them but in the same vein), or are they way out in left field?

You have the final say in your reality. Yes, life happens and there is divine intervention, but what you do with your free will matters. This is why God/the universe doesn't always respond right away when you ask a question. He/it wants to see what you're going to do first. Don't let someone else's insecurities or shortcomings be your north star or compass. Get away from unfruitful negativity. The best way to become is to be, and the best way to be is by doing so without feeling as though you are walking on eggshells. Or you can walk on those eggshells with confidence and not be afraid to break them.

CHAPTER 16

You are You

You are you. In fact, you are so you that there will never be another you. You are unique in that everything that makes you, you, can't be replicated. Imitated sure. Derived from, probably. But one to one, apple to apple, and orange to orange is impossible. One time I had this friend of a friend come at me a little crazy. He was salty that me and the actual friend had been friends for years and were pretty close. One day towards the end of me and that friend's friendship, the friend of the friend must have been feeling himself and said to both of us, "I'm the new Ken now."

Firstly, I can't help but chuckle a little writing that in hindsight because it was like, what? My immediate response to him was, "but you're you." Imitation may be the sincerest form of flattery, but flattery has boundaries. Years later here I am still me. Still black, still healthy by the grace of God, and still making my dreams a reality. I don't know where that young man is today, but I hope he is well, and has come to grips with his own insecurities.

I'm going to go *there* for a quick second: no matter how much you try to change you or try to be something else other than yourself, that will not cause someone who is predisposed to not liking you to start. In life you may come across people that for whatever reason will not like you. You didn't do anything to them, you may hardly know each other, but they have made it up in their mind that even if you gave them $100,000 with no strings attached, they would take it and still curse your name. They just don't like you.

It's not your job to cater to the irresoluteness of public opinion. The same people who will drool over you today will hang you high and stretch you wide tomorrow. Your focus should be authenticity. How much of you are you? Where are you on your journey towards self-actualization? What are you self-actualizing? Are you positive/healthy from an identity formation and capacity fulfillment perspective, or are you corrupt/maladapted?

When you can manage to be the fullness of yourself (in a positive and healthy way), you can also experience alignment. Getting the various aspects of yourself on one accord is easier when you are integrated/not living beneath your potential for maladapted purposes. This is valuable because when you are living in alignment you can't fake the funk. Being aligned with yourself will not allow for dissonance in thought and behavior. You intuitively live out what you think and believe.

If your mind, body, and spirit say go left but your will says go right you're living out of alignment. But when your mind, body, and spirit say go left, and you're willing to go left too, then you are living in alignment. It's integrity on steroids, you're not just behaving a certain way, but you're believing your behavior, and your behavior is fortifying your beliefs. It's a positive feedback loop.

The best thing you can be is yourself. But that also means that you must embrace who you are. This doesn't mean you have to accept who you are; you can decide to change for the better. But even that decision to change should be one of great internal resolve. You don't have to live with someone else's baggage, but you also must be willing to put the bags down. Some of the turmoil you may experience in life can be self-caused. Getting better is a choice. Accepting things and making excuses for the things you are accepting is a slave mentality. Things aren't that difficult you just don't want to get better.

Instead of being drama filled, be peace filled. Sure, outside factors can contribute negatively to certain things, but you are the pilot of your own physiology. No one controls whether or not you catch an attitude, you choose to. No one controls whether or not you are miserable, you choose to be. In the face of difficultly you must find some wherewithal. Find some conviction of spirit that will encourage you to respect your human dignity.

Don't just lay down and die. Don't be afraid to die, but also don't wait for death to come. You will kill your future before it even starts by being immobilized by fear. Some people aren't afraid to be themselves, but rather they are afraid of themselves. Some people are too fearful to be and walk in the fullness of who they really are.

You shouldn't commit philosophical suicide just because you are too afraid of change or failure. Your character has to be developed. Who you are as a person must be refined. That's a lifelong journey. But it's one of the best journeys you can take. You decide what logically makes more sense: doing nothing with your life before you die. Or doing something with your life before you die. In both cases you die. But in one scenario you remain perpetually down on your luck, while in the other, you end up becoming everything you dreamed of and imagined, and more.

The key to your success is walking in your truth with boldness. Once you become confident and comfortable with being you things won't necessarily be smooth sailing all the time. But regardless of the conditions of your context, you can remain resolute in the fact that, who you are as a person is not dependent on the metaphorical (or literal) forecast of the day. Nor is it dependent on whether things go your way all the time. Authenticity produces stability. Choose to be stable.

CHAPTER 17

Self-commodification

With the advent of Artificial Intelligence or AI and the conditions of late-stage capitalism, more and more workers are being left out of the proverbial camp. Being a contributing member of society in some countries is becoming or has become the new ideal. In America for example, the American Dream has historically been a house (with a fence if you are aspirational), a spouse, two and a half kids, a dog, and two cars. It's unfortunate to say that in some respects that dream has become a pipe dream. The new dream by the product of several contributing factors is to be able to effectively contribute what you have to offer and be compensated respectfully for doing so.

Greed in high places has eroded human dignity. If you can't afford an emergency expense or enjoy the fruits of your labor in some capacity, you are missing out in part if not in whole on the meaning of life. And regardless of how subjective you think the meaning of life is, the common denominator for a plurality of people on this topic is to be able to experience some degree of happiness as often as possible.

Happiness not mattering, as some individuals may like to parrot, is antithetical to what it means to be a human. Anyone who says happiness doesn't matter or isn't important is gaslighting you. The Overton window of success keeps moving to the right at the expense of one, the people who actually create wealth through skill and ability; and two, the concept of a modest lifestyle. "Brand" oligopoly has eviscerated people's creativity, curiosity, and mobility.

Your favorite coffee shop having multiple brick and mortars in your local downtown, for example, comes at the cost of your friend not being able to keep his coffee shop in business. Which by consequence causes wealth to leave your community or at the very least not be reinvested in your community in a constructive way. This ultimately makes you and your community poorer. But at least you can get the satisfaction from the feeling that comes with the social status of buying coffee from a "respected" oligarch. This isn't to say that you are an unsupportive friend, though maybe you are, but rather people have become unnaturally inclined to accept whatever is put in front of them, even though what tends to be put in front of you, as a default, doesn't intuitively have your best interest in mind (in that same coffee scenario if you spend those same dollars at your friend's coffee shop, you support a local business and your community. That allows your dollars to circulate locally making it more likely that money will come back to you in one form or another. This makes you richer over time. It also satisfies your need for status by making you an investor where your dollars will go further, a better friend and professional, and several other things associated with being a positively or healthy self-actualized person).

All our lives skepticism and wonder is assaulted with the end goal of trying to extract it from us. From an early age the powers that be try to limit your individuality. You're not allowed to have a dissenting opinion otherwise you run the risk of being ostracized by society. If you don't at least demonstrate that you can think a certain way, you will not receive the passing grade, or you will be passed by when it comes time for a promotion at work. In a pre-modern society world, that same person who you can't stand for their political views may have been your significant other.

An innate inability to be critical or think critically is not authentic human behavior. How people have historically formed bonds and united together has been usurped in the name of profit. Besides the fact that profit tends to trickle up to a select few, the other problem with this is that it's irrational. People can't be governed, inclined to relate to one another, within the context of money, material wealth, and profit, then lose access to those things or find it difficult to acquire for themselves. 10 people can't consume more than 1000 people no matter how big of an appetite they have. So why is it right then for those 10 to hoard all those goods? The same goods by the way that the 1000 probably did the most to contribute to. You contribute to the erosion of your own ecology when you perpetuate anti-human and anti-group ideologies like these.

Rationalizing harm to a multitude of people in the name of preservation and advancement for a few is the doctrine of demons. This is done for the aforementioned of status, the fear of death, and an inherent lack of talent. I have come across several members of the bourgeoisie (true capitalists and the people who carry water for them) who at least share a couple of the same qualities: they don't really do anything with their time on a daily basis, and they lack the ability to transform raw materials in a significant way. If you were to give them wood, nails, a saw, and a hammer, they wouldn't be able to make a table or a stool (this is a generalization and doesn't apply to everyone who falls within the broader topic). This is what makes wealth that is controlled by a few and a capitulation to that, a demonic thought process. Demons are aligned with the devil. The devil is uncreative and can never surpass God, only imitate and unsuccessfully replicate him. Therefore, if you can't successfully copy it, or make a better version for yourself, the only other option is to take it. Economics isn't just a money and politics concern, it's an ideology concern.

Certain people would rather abdicate agency rather than hone their craft or anything about themselves for that matter. They don't want to do it for themselves because either they can't or are lazy. This is why ideas are said to want to be free, but I think they would rather be valuable. A free idea is an idea that anyone can use. This is why your savvy creator or entrepreneur may say that it's not about the idea, it's about the execution. At the same time however, I think that not every idea wants to be over executed either. Just because anyone could try doesn't mean anyone should. If the idea was given to you it was meant for you. That means something. No matter how much someone else tries to take it from you. They may emulate but only you can effectively innovate because you were given the vision.

Does this mean that a creator economy is the only way forward? It shouldn't have to be. The struggle is against pride in high places. Certain people don't want to humble themselves. Certain industries are afraid of Moloch. Instead of turning away from pride, greed, lust, envy, wrath, gluttony, and sloth-ness, people will allow themselves to become conduits for these sins and amplify the behavior associated with them. This hurts regular people who while hardworking, aren't necessarily inclined to create and market a product. What about your average John and Jane Doe's? These are the people society is trying to box and faze out. But at the same time these are the people who are the economic drivers of any society. There will always be more of them than anyone else.

Self-commodification is about retaining your economic and consequently societal viability. It's survival. This theme has come up several times now but that just shows you how existential being able to see a new sunrise every morning is, or at least has become over time. A commodity is a raw material. You must become a need. The proverbial they should feel the need to compensate you appropriately because without you, things won't run as smoothly, if at all. This is the same thing the bourgeoisie does. The only difference is the bourgeoisie don't really contribute anything to the group at large, besides owning the means of production. That makes their perceived importance and influence inflated and conflated.

Become the local expert in your skill and craft. The good thing about being the expert is the expert gets paid. Things can imitate the expert, but the expert will always be one of a kind. Things need the expert; the expert doesn't need things. The way AI works for example is that it's ability to generate prompts is based off what is coded into it. The base code for primitive AGI comes from an amalgamation of human knowledge both copyrighted and in the public domain. Without all that information from experts and with the realization thereof, AI loses its allure. Anyone and anything can copy, but it takes something special to create something new. Creativity can't be authentically coded.

This is what gives you an edge in a society that is trying to make you obsolete. Hyper authenticity through refined genuineness makes you stand out in a crowd. There is nothing intrinsically wrong with the crowd itself, it's just that the people that the crowd trusts to lead them, is leading them off a cliff. The profit motive doesn't care about the long term because it assumes its perpetual existence. Profit thinks profit isn't going anywhere. And while there is a certain truth to that, anything that isn't taken care of won't last. The means and lens through which society values profit is dismissive. Money is the byproduct of profit. Profit is the value in the communication between two individuals. Profit is the meaning that comes forth within the context of an exchange. Those who mishandle profit think or act as though profit is money and that the value that produces that money doesn't intrinsically matter.

The uncreative don't understand the impact that having a need fulfilled has. Those who are philistines by genetic lineage or operate under a certain ideology either don't realize or don't themselves value what it means for someone to experience a moment of happiness, relief, peace, and the like. Imagine you're a parent, maybe you are, I don't know it to be true, but I can guess that finding a good babysitter on date night with your spouse or so that you can handle business for a few hours, is an alleviation and a comfort. That feeling and experience matters though some nouns may not agree.

When you commodify yourself you make what matters to you valuable. This comes through work, effort, and determination. You've got to want it for yourself, and you've got to want to be good at it. If you can find your niche and excel in it, you will position yourself for doors to regularly open for you. People still like people. And people aren't going anywhere. The less accessible wealth becomes the less important it will become. If the same 10 people mentioned earlier have all the resources, the 1000 people will just find a new resource. Status isn't as important as you think it is or as meaningful as you may want it to be.

In an anarchical society Joe Doe probably would give less than two thoughts about Joe Not-Shmoe Esq. the Third of the House of Shmoely Descendant of the Shmoéleesians, Ph.D MBA CPA DDS BSN LPC PCP LMSW PMHNP-BC. The more people's access to self-determination gets degraded the more individuals will begin to buy out of society. Human dignity needs to be treated with respect from the top down. And if society won't respect you, you must respect you. Get more out of your life by not allowing the meaning to be drained from your life.

CHAPTER 18

Keep Hope Alive

Keeping hope alive is a materially ineffective pursuit. What contributes to the impotency of keeping hope alive is the nature of hope itself. Hope is passive. Typically said in finance in reference to trading the market, but also used elsewhere, is that hope is not a strategy. Hoping is losing. Once you start hoping it's time to sell (proverbially, not financial advice). Now there are redeeming qualities to hope and hoping, but generally speaking it's important that your hope is put in its proper place.

I would argue that far more valuable than hope is justice. Justice is active. Justice can be pursued in the here and now. You don't have to wait for someone to give you justice. You can demand justice. You can march for justice. When you notice an injustice, you can speak out against it, in pursuit of justice. These two things are far less semantical than it appears. Justice is fair or right treatment; hope is a feeling...

Hope is a feeling of expectation and a desire for something to happen. While you're feeling for an expectation someone else is out in the streets demanding that expectation. That's the issue with hope. It can encourage ineptitude. Hope is really good for getting a lot of amens and riling up a crowd, but when that moment passes and it's time for the real work to begin, you don't just need hope, you also need a plan. Then once you have a plan you need action. People aren't taking action like they used to.

It's easy to get inspired but inspiration and conformity, or comfort for that matter, don't yield anything. I used to work for this sales company in New York, and it was rough. It was door to door, and how I got to cut my teeth coming up in my career. Every morning, before they sent us out to our various territories we would have a sales team meeting. The meeting was to get people hyped up and excited about the day's work, and to highlight various benchmarks of success. The morning meeting would often be very energetic, people would be cheering, the sales managers would be pontificating, and everyone was bought in for the first 15 minutes of every day. But then the real work would start.

The reason the morning meetings were so electrifying was because the work was so demanding and daunting. There were some people at this job who liked the morning meeting more than doing the work. We called those people "juice monkeys." They were only there for the juice. They just wanted the hype. In the same way there are some people who are all in on hope but disappear when it comes to the necessary work.

I was on the football team at my high school. Playing football in high school always comes with some fandom. I remember that my coach at the time would frequently inform us to not get caught up in what he would call the "rah, rah." The assemblies, parades, award ceremonies, team dinners and the like; all meant nothing if there was no meaningful work behind it. If we weren't winning games, it didn't matter how excited we got off the field.

This is what can happen when you "keep hope alive." You get so caught up in the rah, rah of hope while being impotent as it relates to what's required to hope. The Bible says that faith is the substance of things hoped for and the evidence of things not seen. If you're hoping that means you are utilizing faith. The Bible also says that faith without work is dead. You can't have meaningful faith that isn't backed by any action on your part. Therefore, you also can't have real hope without the same. Like a lot of things in life, hope has been neutered. The essence of hope has been removed, made rudimentary, and or discarded. Keeping hope alive has become hope's SOS.

Another hard truth is that some people aren't ever really inclined to hope. People are social beings and talk is cheap. It's easy to say you have hope. People will pretend to be hopeful to be included. But if you allow hope to be hope then what you may come across is a bunch of people who were never really about being hopeful or having hope. They had hope until someone said let's go do this or go do that. But action that's the true essence of hope.

If you're going to keep hope alive you must stand up. Again, while you're feeling, someone else is doing. Hope in essence requires work. Hope in theory is ethereal. And while the ethereal is nice, in church communities you'll hear it said, that you don't want to be so heavenly minded that you are of no earthly good. Stop defanging hope. Apply some faith or work-backed belief to what you are hoping for. That's where the results are and that's where change is. Don't just talk about it, be about it.

CHAPTER 19

Own Your Own Stuff

There is a positive correlation between ownership and wealth. Objectively speaking, the more you own the wealthier you are. This is why we have terms like "production" and "means of production." Means of production implies ownership. You own the tools and resources necessary for the creation of goods and or services. Production is creation. Creation and means for creation, the tools necessary thereof, have been separated as a way to control wealth. Your average person in the 21st century doesn't own the means of production for their labor.

And with subscription models certain entrepreneurs may never truly own the means of production for their labor either and will just be permanent renters. This is a clear example of late-stage capitalism. The haves keep the have nots from having but then give them hopium and copium.

What you create is valuable but if you're an average worker within the context of a corporate structure specifically, not exclusively, you miss out on that value every day because you don't at least share in ownership of the means of production, let alone own them yourself.

This separation of creation and ownership is an age-old issue that has failed in some cases north of 70% of a general populous. If an economic system only benefits the top 20-30% anecdotally, and only the top 5% materially, then it isn't one that benefits workers. There will always be more workers than any other segment in an economic structure. The question is whether those workers can retain at least a greater portion of the wealth generated from their work (if not all of it).

I've learned that you can't on face value do something for someone else, give that someone else the fruit of your labor, and expect that someone else to turn around and give you back a notable portion of that fruit either directly, or translated in some form of compensation. It's also not necessarily ethical (or possible) to tax that fruit prior to delivery.

If you are not in control of (own) the means of production for your labor, the things required for your work to be completed, then your claim to the profits generated from your work is diminished. If this circumstance applies to you than it can be argued that you are not a capitalist, but rather merely a participant in a capitalist system. For a capitalist the end goal is capital or profits. Ownership in general but specifically of the means of production is how that is acquired. People who are hired to use the means of production or oversee those who do, are the somewhat inconvenient middle people "required" for the generation of wealth. The problem is there are more of those people than there are true capitalists or members of the bourgeoisie.

The capitalist system in its current form as of the pinning of this book can be perfidious. The micro can be extrapolated to the macro and just like a capitalist owns the means of production relative to their industry, they also, put loosely, own the means of production relative to governance. Capitalism as a political and economic system is inclined to work, with capitalists at the top of the hierarchy. The fact of the matter is capitalism is the best economic system the world has ever known up to this point. The problem is in how it's organized.

The value of ownership is the only thing anyone really has. An asset can appreciate. It can be liquidated. It can be utilized. They can be passed down. They can be collected. They can also be multiplied as well as diversified. If you don't have an asset, you don't really own anything. And if you have an asset that can be taken away from you then you don't own that asset.

Ownership is something to strive for at every level, morally, materially, and otherwise. Renting in perpetuity is not the natural state of healthy economics. Wealth can't proliferate or grow meaningfully if people aren't empowered by their own self-determination to create new streams of revenue. Renting and laboring kills creativity in most fruitful ways that don't include corporate politics. But creativity is the only true means of real revenue generation AKA wealth.

The problem is, as mentioned in chapter 17, twofold. On the one hand, generally speaking, the bourgeoisie and members of the managerial class are inherently uncreative. They fundamentally can't make anything. They don't have the wherewithal to transform raw materials and they don't value the value of creativity. Creativity to these people is a means to an end and not the end itself. On the other hand, there is the spiritual influences of greed and Moloch. Greed is a sin focused on the selfish desire for materially impactful resources. Desires are generally God given good things. However, greed is a perversion in that it's a selfish desire. Not one with origins in divine purity, but rather one birthed out of carnal influences limited nearly exclusively to one's own motives, without selfless consideration of others and to the material things of the world.

Moloch is an ancient god that people historically would sacrifice to for wealth and prosperity. The implication or idea of Moloch in a capitalist society is that this deity specializes in pitting people and industries against one another. With the advent of a new idea or new technology, the influence of Moloch suggests that if you don't keep up with a certain pace of research and development, and production, you may end up losing [market share] to the competition. The catch is this is a perversion and provocation of innate human interests in a way that leads to material arms races and the inevitable destruction of all parties involved.

Having and being able to beat competition is valuable, but it shouldn't be existential. It only becomes existential in a profit-motivated system and structure. Market share matters to capitalists because that's how capitalists generate capital; by selling goods or services, having people to sell their goods or services to. And or by acquiring money from investors. This is how people have evolved to survive to a certain degree. People are generally inclined to not want to live in a way that doesn't ensure a certain level of longevity and stability. The underpinning for this reality within the context of a "modern" agriculture-based civilization is one that includes the free flow of capital. The perversion of this is when people choose to live selfishly. Cash is always moving, and it enjoys going to the top. While self-preservation is important, the responsibility of those at the top of a hierarchy is to at least make it easier for those at the bottom, if not engage in wealth redistribution. Selfishness is anti-human.

Throughout this book so far, I've highlighted some of the motives of individuals who choose to live in a way that is anti-human, and they generally boil down to survival and security (or a lack or inability thereof). Essentially those people choose to be less human because they are insecure in some capacity, and they want to ensure survival. Ensuring survival in a pro-human way tends to require a certain kind of work and generates results that people may believe to be antiquated and or undesirable. Even though those results are more fulfilling. It's important to remember that some people don't have the capacity to take care of themselves. These individuals lack creativity and ability, but they still exist and need to figure something out for themselves. Often times proliferating a harmful system to meet their selfish needs and desires is how they cope with their insecurities from their inability to demonstrate a hard skill or survival skills.

These people typically aren't happy with their life, but they have things and status which in their mind make up for their shortcomings, at least partially. These people would rather perpetuate disintegration than learn how to do something constructive. The prospect of being a better person is unappealing to them. They don't want to and or can't conceive to [do the work necessary to] contribute to life and society in a healthy and positive way. These are the same people who tend to make it far in certain societal structures. They do the bidding of malevolent forces for their own wealth and prosperity. The minority who tries to ruin or distort something for the majority are devil and or Moloch worshipers, pro-demon and or studiers and followers of demon doctrine, and or at the very least maladapted or corrupted.

Getting your mind right means putting yourself in a position to survive in a pro-human way. You do that by developing hard skills. When you develop a hard skill, you are doing what is required to become self-actualized/experience self-actualization. Being able to contribute to something in a material way is what will give your life purpose and meaning. The steps to not being maladapted, disintegrated, corrupted, pro-demon, or animalistic, are practical, pragmatic, and available to you.

One of the concerns you may have with this reality is that healthy self-actualization "takes longer," or doesn't necessarily guarantee a lavish life. I empathize with this point of descent. The truth is what's in you is meant to come forth through you. If you can identify a desire to be materially wealthy as one that is divinely or celestially imbued in you, then it will happen for you, one way or another, if you put the work in that is necessary. Additionally, being maladapted may not be beneficial for you. If the "fast way" to your God given desires requires you to sacrifice your character in away your convictions are opposed to, it either won't work or won't last. You may have been taught that if you do all the things "right," then you'll have the success you want. The issue if you're like me is, that whoever told you what the "right way" was, didn't effectively mention the terms and conditions of that lifestyle. If you've been doing the "right" thing, you went to school, earned your education and or have been a good and hard worker, have faithed based values around family, exhibit self-control, pay your bills on time, so on and so forth, and you still find yourself meandering through life nebulously, then that "right way" is maladaptive and not right for you. The sooner you break out of living maladaptively, the sooner you can put yourself in a position to better achieve and experience your desires and the success you want.

It's possible to be benevolent and resourceful, proliferating wealth in a more equal and generous way. This looks like a market where individuals and corporations have the ability to generate wealth, pay workers respectable wages, engage in healthy competition and optimization, grow in a measured way that doesn't lead to economic upheaval for employees, and not use greed as an ethical business practice. Generally, though not conclusively, those individuals who tend to own the means of production reinforce the perverse feedback loop certain entities like to provoke among people in various spaces, places, and capacities. And instead of regulating those kinds of negative incentives so that the measure of success isn't profits, pay raises to CEOs, or stock buybacks for shareholders, individuals in seats of power and change tend to sell out to these and similar forces.

Objectively, no one should want to return to the state of nature, where people are surviving in a more visceral way. That being said, the state of nature is where everything comes from and eventually returns to; and the values of that plain of existence help keep people together. When societies stop working for the majority of their citizens, the people at the top who govern said societies (or fail to do so) are complicit in their downfall. Ultimately this is what deities like the devil and Moloch want and because of their shrewdness they can disguise it as, a limited regulation free market system intended to benefit everyone. These forces work together and lead to people doing things that are disconnected from the general well-being of humanity as a whole. This is a doctrine or ideology of demons, deriving from and or of the devil himself.

The doctrine of demons is a Judeo-Christian understanding of an ideological approach to hating the things of God and in particular, humans. The devil, or Satan, is the originator of this ideology from when he first rebelled against God in Heaven. He thought he could exalt himself above God and convinced one third of Heaven's inhabitants that he could. Somewhere during his failed coup attempt, God decided to create humans. I am taking this detour to shed light on some of the invisible forces on, in, and around your life. Humans from a theological and spiritual perspective represent a unique aspect of God that the devil can't achieve, replication. The devil can't reproduce or procreate. From a biblical perspective humans are the image bearers of God. The devil can't make anything substantively; but he can influence. Since his first interaction with Eve in the Garden of Eden, the devil has spread his ideology of hate and contempt for humans throughout the world just like Jesus tells his disciples to spread the gospel. The devil hates what he can't have. He can't be God and he can't create. Hating humans and convincing us to self-harm on a macro and micro level manifests in a plethora of ways.

Demons don't want humans to own their own things because demons hate humans. AI, while I'm not necessarily completely opposed to it, is a great example of this. AI takes an amalgamation of human knowledge and uses code to shuffle that information around to "think" and produce responses. Then the uncreative bourgeoisie [try to] use that technological advancement to increase their profits at the expense of human laborers. Then either they themselves or a member of the managerial class within their specific organization or subjective field, who isn't as in danger of losing their economic viability say things like, "because of AI people will have jobs that haven't even been thought of yet."

This also is a good representation of Moloch and greed because the people making these decisions want more material goods: money, power, homes, and other resources, and are influenced in believing that if they don't out pace other AI developers, they will end up losing their own economic viability. And in the end, if and when all of this inevitably leads to artificial super intelligence that can bypass all of the "safety features" humans' program into it, the only one who really wins is Moloch AKA the devil and his demons.

Capitalism and hyper-industrialization are directed by the influences of the ideologies of the nouns that oversee them. This can make the experience of these things detrimental, but not necessarily the concepts themselves. You can either concern yourself with the benevolence of a demon, or you can tap into your God given ability and work towards materializing things that can't be easily taken away from you if at all, and that have a dividend or appreciate in some way. All the while working towards a better reality not just for yourself but for others as well. Take a proactive approach to things that don't just insulate you from the problem, but that also eliminate the problem, or at least don't perpetuate it, and makes it easier for those coming behind you.

CHAPTER 20

How to Shift Your View on Success to Obtain it Regularly

Do you have limiting beliefs that are inhibiting your breakthroughs and or blocking your ability to have success? A limiting belief is a belief or thought process that puts a lid on your capabilities. It's when you believe or rationalize certain things about yourself and or context that may be keeping you from your desires. What exacerbates this is if you accept that thought or perpetuate that mindset across your reality. Do you struggle with being the person you genuinely want to be? Have you ever wished that you had the same level of courage as someone else who is doing what you would like to be doing? If you can channel that energy and vitality properly, you can attain the level of success you desire.

The traditional view of success is materialism.

Objectively speaking when you ask an average person what success is, they are likely to say a nice car, a house, a good paying job, a beautiful spouse etc. While those things can be an indication of success, what makes someone successful goes deeper than the number of bills they have to pay per month, or the assets and liabilities on their balance sheet. Success doesn't just have to be things. It can also be meaning and a personally enjoyable high quality of life. Quality of life refers to how you live on a daily basis. And while this doesn't necessarily exclude material things, it's not primarily focused on those accoutrements either.

You must overcome your mental barriers. Anything worth having is worth pursuing. The only way you fail is if you quit. Suspend your unbelief and start asking yourself, "why not me and why not now?" Can you envision your compelling future? Success is about living in the fullness of yourself and allowing your passions to inform your identity.

It's important to position yourself in a way where success is drawn to you. In challenging times, it can be tough to see the light at the end of the tunnel; however, it's important that you know that there is always one there. Sometimes the challenge people have in their pursuit of success is that they allow themselves to get distracted and sidetracked. People can get so caught up in the day to day that they lose their drive.

You can't lose determination if you're serious about achieving something in and with your life. You must know your "why." Your why is your motivation, your hope, and the reason you get out of bed every day. It's your responsibility to yourself to see that light at the end of the tunnel. Your setbacks are just setups for your comebacks. In those instances, you are in a position to have a breakthrough!

A breakthrough is a sudden circumstance change in

your favor. As a result, what was once impeding you is no longer opposition for you. Sometimes a breakthrough can materialize and sometimes it's a change in perspective. The value in a breakthrough is the impact it has on your perception. A breakthrough will renew your hope. One of the breakthroughs that led me to the point of pinning this book was realizing I had my number one commodity back, which is time, after being laid off due to Covid-19. And in addition to that, I never wanted to sell my time for less than what I valued it to be worth ever again.

What is that thing that you want to attain? And are you in a place to receive it? You shift your view on success by giving yourself the right to be successful. You have to want yourself to achieve something. And that thing that you want to achieve should be considerate of others. Showing gratitude and humility is a key ingredient in perpetuating success. Success is portrayed through money and things; it's not defined by them. Success is a byproduct of your developed character traits and behaviors.

Big victories are not big because of their scale and scope. Big victories are big because of the preparation that comes before the opportunity. The equation to success is hard work plus luck. When you are engaging in successful

habits those habits will make room for you to encounter bigger opportunities to excel in and serve others. The reality is, success does not come rapidly nor is it always grandiose, but it can come consistently.

Success Rooted in Discipline

An example of a successful person is someone who

starts their day by making their bed. Making your bed every day puts you in a place to be successful because you will have already accomplished something when you first wake up. If you can accomplish one task at the start of your day, you will engage inertia and be more inclined to want to accomplish more. And while how you quantify your success should not be tethered to your ability to accomplish a task, the value of your success should be in the meaning of that task being accomplished. Why would a person find value in making their bed in the morning? Because at the very least, at the end of a long day you know you have a made bed waiting for you.

By shifting your focus from success that's rooted in superficial things and results that may be void personal buy in, to success that's rooted in disciplined activities and systems that lead to desired results; you will begin to see constant success and will create for yourself opportunities to be successful on a larger scale. I engage in generating consistent success for myself by doing things that I am passionate about. If you are passionate about something the success will come. Passion drives motivation, motivation drives discipline, discipline drives determination and determination drives success. Put a system in place for what you are interested in. Stop treating your happiness as a second-class citizen in your own life. Don't just find time for the things you don't want to do and call them "responsibilities;" but also make time for the things you do want to do and that will make you better as a person and your existence more vivid.

If you are not willing to get better at something, then that something isn't your passion. Start making small yet intentional behavioral changes that connect you with what matters to you. For me that looked like working out consistently, reading regularly, and creating space for the things I value. Also utilize accountability partners to assist in keeping you on track and focused. This is the healthy self-actualization that will keep you from being disintegrated or intentionally hurting others. You must be willing to strive for what you value because it won't always come naturally, and even if it does, it still needs to be developed.

Success is available to everyone, and you can achieve it by first operationally defining it (explicitly stating what it is you want). Secondly, by adopting disciplined and intentional actions in the areas of your life that are most meaningful to you and will contribute to you experiencing your desired results. Let your passions drive you to a place of abundance and gratitude and position you to receive and be the catalyst for breakthrough opportunities. Remember, there is a light at the end of the tunnel, the question is whether you are willing to go towards it.

CHAPTER 21

Skills

Sometimes it can feel as though "everyone" has the silver bullet except you. The proverbial everyone seems to be able to find some groundbreaking way to generate a lot of income fast, while despite your efforts, you're struggling to find a higher salary or an opportunity to get the next level position in your field; or to sell your own goods and services. During the pandemic, within my sphere of influence, it seemed to me as though everyone was buying a house, getting debt free, becoming well off from trading the stock market, advancing to the next stage in their life, so on and so forth. Meanwhile there I was having a challenging time keeping a dollar. Contextually things ended up playing out well for me in that season of my life, but the point is that in some moments, it can feel as though you are falling behind or not "where you should be" within the context of your contemporaries, people part of your decadal era, or in life in general. One time I saw a post about a teenager who was earning six figures while still in high school. The profile who made that post tried to use the story as motivation when in reality if true, it would have been a very far outlier. When you see stories about certain people prospering in some of the aforementioned and similar ways, it's a good thing to take a trust but verify approach.

While I was in undergrad one of my professors once said during a class that, you should never lose your skepticism and wonder. The value of this kind of mindset is that it allows you to be jubilant for someone else's successes, while at the same time humble, and considerate of your own circumstances. The fact of the matter is the grass isn't always greener on the other side, and you may not be willing or have the ability to do what someone else had to, to get their [proverbial] grass to look so green. And the last thing you should want is to get caught up in some scam.

When you see and read about other people's successes and or things that appear to be lucrative, there can be this inherent initial response to want to believe or buy into that narrative. This is how the sentiment about certain people and doing certain things to become successful spreads. Several people begin to believe and talk about the success of a person, place, or thing, and then that noun's association with success becomes real because people make it real. The veneer of success tends to outshine the reality thereof, and some nouns like to manipulate that duplicity for themselves. Perception informs reality and we are all liable to buy into a non-reality. I have done it before and it's not always about getting rich quick.

Sometimes you want something new and or you are tired of being disillusioned with the facts of your life. Despite life being in favor of you, you can still face objectively difficult situations. In these moments you may want to find an escape or some way to alleviate the stress that challenge has brought with it. It's times like these and similar ones where you may be more susceptible to believing a "life changing story or opportunity," that ends up being a farce. The quicker you realize that you can't escape your life's challenges that you need to conquer and learn from, the better off you'll be. Even if you manage to avoid a hardship or obstacle in one season of your life, that same or a similar difficulty will likely appear in another.

You can do the right thing in the wrong place. The road to hell is paved with good intentions. The reason people can fall for glamorizing another person's life, various scams, deceptive personalities, rags to riches stories, and the like, is because they are not satisfied with their life. The solution to dissatisfaction isn't always radical change, however. You need to get your efforts and your purpose on one accord. Don't use someone else's story as a blueprint for your life. Glean inspiration from it sure, but also affirm the reality that you are your own person and because of your unique identity, no one has ever lived your life before. Getting caught up in a relatively remote story or perception is how you can end up falling for a lie. There are things that are objectively true, then there are things that are true exclusively for you.

If a certain level of success or a behavior is not replicable then it's not scalable. And if it's not scalable then it's a unicorn. One of the attributes of a unicorn is that it's mythical. Some of the success you are exposed to is more a byproduct of luck than it is work ethic. Don't base your interpretation of your life on the luck of something or someone else. And if and when people tell you that you aren't successful at something because you have a production problem (you aren't working hard enough), they are gaslighting you.

Hard work is important and it's what makes luck work and meaningful. That being said however, some people are luckier than others in certain contexts. Take the lottery for example. While on one hand you may have to be in it to win it, on the other hand the odds of winning a large jackpot are usually less than getting struck by lightning. If you're not lucky enough to get struck by lightning on any given day, are you all that willing to test your luck and waste resources on something even less likely? Opportunities come to everyone, but some people have objectively better ones at one time or another. That doesn't mean you can't create your own luck (i.e. a breakthrough moment) but it does highlight the fact that hard work isn't the sole contributor to getting the most out of your life. But if you do have a production problem then that's something you should address. You must be able to strike a healthy balance between working as hard as you can, while also submitting to the fact that in certain situations there is nothing more you can do, and some luck, or a miracle, is in order.

As someone who has worked in a corporate sales setting for a notable amount of time, I am all too familiar with quotas. Sales and quotas are flawed in that they don't always account for or frankly care about the absurdity of life. From my experience your average sales leader doesn't care that your target market isn't responding well to what you're selling, or that the business model is busted. Instead, they just tell you to work harder. Anyone who says working harder is the only solution is playing you or is being naive (and some people like to pretend to be naive).

Your hard work is not a printing press. And not to rehash previous chapters, but the worth you receive for your work, especially in an employer-employee context, doesn't always equate fairly to the worth your work actually produces. So, from that perspective it becomes really easy for your leaders to tell you to work harder when they are keeping the lion's share of the byproduct of your efforts. Just because, and this is true of life regardless of context, you don't necessarily see the fruit of your labor, doesn't mean your labor isn't baring fruit. It could be what you're getting for your work is immaterial, or it could be that you are only getting a fraction of what your work produced. Either way it matters that you know and are at peace with what your life energy is going towards because at the end of the day, all you have is how you spend any given 24 hours.

The point here is not getting what you [think you] want from your output doesn't make you less valuable, your purpose less meaningful, your vision less attainable or your desires irrational. Sometimes a better perspective is required. Not everyone's experience in life will be the same. You are not less of a person because it takes you years to do or get what someone else was able to in months.

Here's the other thing, ask yourself: would you be discontent if you didn't know what someone else has or is doing? A lot of your dissatisfaction can come from comparison. Comparing yourself to others is not always your fault though. People are victims to that mentality because when you go on social media all you see is someone's glory and never the literal story of their life. The people you follow on social media are not on a perpetual vacation or free of any challenges; they are just showing you their highlight reel.

Even celebrities are not always glammed up. There is nothing wrong with aspiring to a certain level of success but that should be tempered with a dose of realism. You can be successful and famous, but it may take time. Yes, some people do get things handed to them and or have things come to them more easily; but that's not the norm. Don't despise your lived experience based on the things you don't know about someone else's.

Experience is Real

What you go through matters. Exposure has value. You are more experienced than you think. Experience goes beyond a resume, and it goes beyond how many times you have been around the sun. You must be able to parlay what you go through to your advantage. Not much else matters in life beyond the actualization of your perspicacity.

People start learning while they are still in their mother's womb. As a Fetus you learned how to differentiate sounds. When you were born you learned how to navigate the world. How to walk, to live, and engage with your environment. Those skills aid in socialization and you being able to connect with other humans. From there, pre-kindergarten-High school is 12-14+ years on average of learning. Then that gets built upon as you decide to go to college or trade school, and or into the work force. Once in adulthood everything you do is a culmination of what you gathered on the way to where you are, and what you are continuing to learn. This matters because if you don't place value on what you're exposed to, no one will.

A problem you may be having in relation to utilizing your experience is a lack of confidence. Are you confident in what you have learned from what you have gone through? What did you learn from what you have gone through? Sometimes people tend to not lean on their experience because they associate experience with time or repetitions primarily. This is a fallacy. The average life span of a person is around 75 years old. In the grand scheme of things that isn't that long of a time. A tree can be thousands of years old. Glass Sponges are the oldest animals on earth and can live for 15,000 years. There are even things in life that are eternal.

Most people work for over 40 years before retiring. All professions existed long before you or me. If all you go on is sun revolutions, you miss the point of learning from what you go through. Your experience is supposed to help you become the fullness of your realized potential. Who you become is dependent on what you learn from your experiences. Besides a craft or something you want to become or are an expert in, many times in life you may have a one-off experience. It happened once and has not happened again since. Or it's a once in a lifetime moment that won't happen again. You can't discount these moments.

The only reason not to be confident in your experiences is because you did not learn anything from them. This is a vicious cycle in life. If you don't learn from what you go through you will not see progress in your life. People don't learn because they are either actively opposed to learning (hardheaded) or because they don't value what they are learning.

Just because you don't think something is important doesn't mean that it isn't. And that thing that isn't important to you, might be the thing you need to get where you want to go.

Think of it like a test. In school, if you do not pass the test, then you do not pass the class, and you must take either the test or class over again. In the same way, life is a proverbial school, your experiences are the lessons, and your challenges are the test. If you do not utilize your learning material to help you pass, you will have to take the test/class again (not progress in your life or struggle with the same or similar difficulties and obstacles). And sometimes it is that lesson that you missed or weren't paying as close attention to, that ends up being a determining factor.

In life you will encounter similar or slightly varied situations over time. Have you ever met a person who was just like another person that you stopped associating with? Or maybe you left one place or job thinking that the next one would be better. Only to find out that it was just the same, but with a fresh coat of paint. This is a paradox of life. Nothing is new under the sun, but also, nothing is really all that new to you either. If you took a moment to assess your current situation, I am sure you would find subjective similarities to a previous period or season in your life.

Your call in life isn't to create or seek new experiences for yourself, it's to learn from the existing ones you have. Sometimes you just need to learn to go with the flow. This doesn't mean try to control the context of the flow; it means flowing with the flow. If the flow is smooth, then its smooth sailing. If the flow is rough, then you may be tossed and turned. This is where your experience comes into play. Your experience is there to help you manage the flow. And if you don't like your flow, instead of trying to change that which is serendipitous in your life, change your perspective and approach to it. Free will is most fully expressed in what you do, do (what you affect change upon), and not in what you get to do (what you have the potential to do or not do).

Risk Tolerance

One of the things that is critical as it relates to uncovering your way in your life, is understanding your risk tolerance. Risk tolerance refers to the amount of risk you are willing to expose yourself to. Risk is danger. The amount of danger you are willing to take on influences the degree of success you are likely to see on the other side.

Typically speaking risk tolerance is an investment term. That being said, you can flip that fact on its head and ask yourself, "how invested am I in my own life?" The part not everyone will tell you is, everything is risk. As mentioned in a previous chapter, waking up is a risk. Going outside is a risk. Eating is a risk. Everything you do on a normal day-to-day basis poses some type of danger, perceived or actual. You must find the level of danger with which you are comfortable.

Finding your comfort zone within the danger zone is important because you must be willing to fall victim to that level of danger. In investing for example, let's say you buy or sell a call or put option. The inherent risk in any of those trades is that you could lose the capital or collateral you invest. If you buy shares of a company, you run the risk of that company's stock tanking or plunging in value and you losing your money. The secret to risk tolerance is that you must be okay with the potential unfavorable results associated with a risk.

To change the subject from finance, when you eat a meal for example, you risk choking, someone around you not knowing the Heimlich maneuver or cardiopulmonary resuscitation, having no way to contact emergency services, or you being alone and unable to help yourself, and you dying. When you cross the street, you risk someone running a red light or stop sign and hitting you hard enough to cause irreparable damage.

The good thing about risk, which is why it's perpetual, is that it comes with reward. Every day you are presented with new opportunities, and every time you arrive at one you must ask yourself, "is the risk worth the reward?" Is sustenance worth potentially choking over? Is arriving at a certain location worth possibly being hit by a motor vehicle? Is the money worth your mental health? Are the potential returns on a certain investment worth it? This is called discernment. Discernment is being able to judge for yourself whether or not something is worth its weight in gold (literally or metaphorically).

Your job, your morals, your desires, your relationships, your network, your comfort. How valuable are they? Are they an asset or a liability? Every day you must think about these things and make relevant decisions about them. This is where experience comes in and where finding what works for you is crucial. The best thing you can be every day is yourself. You come with risk. You must rise to your own level of inherent risk if you ever want to amount to anything. You must be willing to do what you must do, not what someone else has to do, to make it. And sometimes what that looks like for your life can be riskier than what that looks like for someone else's life, or what you may be comfortable with. You must decide that you are worth your compelling future.

Your desires have risk. You must accept the risk to materialize the associated rewards. When you know what you want and know how to utilize your skills and experience for that purpose, you can better gauge whether at any given time the risk is worth the reward. Deploy your perspicacity in your favor. Galvanize your knowledge to help you make better decisions. Become confident about the things you know or want to know. Do not obfuscate your mind. This is how you make life tactful and sticky. This is one way you will be able to look back over your life and draw meaningful and content conclusions.

CHAPTER 22

The Threshold

Research shows that the human brain fully develops in your mid to late twenties. Mainly this means your prefrontal cortex fully matures and your ability to critically think solidifies. Your prefrontal cortex is responsible for helping you make "good decisions." I'm not going to discuss good decisions here because of the relative ambiguity of the topic. Contextualized maturity is of value here however, because so many factors contribute to how you make decisions. Aside from know-how there is also context-your phenotypical influences.

All of us are byproducts of our genetic make-up, and the context thereof. Who your parents are and how they live contribute greatly to your ability to excel. Based on luck of cosmic draw or predestination, whichever you prefer, you may have to make more difficult or critical decisions as it relates to what your life means to you. Genetics to a certain degree can be overcome or mitigated, but context can hold you back indefinitely.

This is why guiding principles are so valuable. When you believe in and for something, that will inform your everyday life both proverbially and practically. If you are of a certain belief system, that belief system will guide your decisions in real time. That is, you actively contributing to the creation of your reality. Depending on what your belief system is, there will be certain things that your convictions won't allow you to stand for or condone. Again, in those moments that is also an active participation on your part in the creation of your reality.

Decisions are tacky. They stick and materialize in the most literal sense of the word. When you do something, you are doing something. Your doing something is a manifestation and materialization. When you are doing things, things are being done. Things are becoming matter. That's why faith without work is dead. Because without the work nothing materializes. And objectively you can't or don't really have hope for something you aren't materializing (working for). Being able to make thoughtful decisions matters because if you aren't taking effective steps towards a vision, purpose, or ideology, then you aren't going anywhere in and with your life.

Vision, calling, and other philosophical and existential experiences like these matter because they contribute to your life's trajectory. You aren't going to do much of anything with your life if you don't see yourself doing so. Your desires cling onto experiences. You can have a want but if that want doesn't appear to be feasible to you, then that want likely won't happen. Riding a roller-coaster tends to be less scary after you've already ridden a few. Driving may be intimidating when you are first learning, but eventually it can become second nature. Becoming acclimated or exposed to certain things is a blessing.

Once you know what good food tastes like you won't want bad food on purpose. What you experience can give your desires the scope, breadth, and depth they need to flourish and expand. You didn't know you wanted a pool at your house until you visited someone who had one, now you're coming up with a plan to materialize it. You may not have known how differently people can live until you left your hometown. What you believe can influence what you see, and what you see can influence where you want to go.

Not everyone is privy to certain revelations. You must be willing to allow yourself to think differently and dynamically. Embrace moments in life where you suspend your unbelieve and let go of your preconceived notions. Some people come from an environment where they are exposed to various things and are encouraged to explore and forge their own path. And some people need help in getting exposure or they need a seed planted in their mind that encourages exploration. Life must be birthed and or cultivated in you. Life in this sense refers to vitality, awe and wonder, curiosity, and drive. It's your willingness to want. It's not enough to have a desire, what also matters is the degree at which you want said desire. Do you really want what you [think or believe you] want, and how badly do you want it?

That's not always taught, nor does it always come naturally. Sometimes it requires divine intervention. And this is where maturity and effective decision making come into play. Once you know what the right decision is you can work towards making it happen. Again, that right decision for you is likely subjective, but whatever it is, once you come to it, and there usually isn't multiple within the context of your desires, you must decide to execute. Your phenotype may not always contribute to you knowing what the correct way to execute is, but nothing beats exposure as it relates to knowing what type of execution styles are available. And in your process of uncovering the way in which you want to do something, you'll see where doing something that way could lead you. That is vision. That is hope.

CHAPTER 23

Focus

Focus is one of if not your most powerful attribute. What you focus on you materialize. This is similar to Law of Attraction. Focus is centering your attention on and or around something. This is valuable because your attention creates your reality. The content of your focus isn't as salient as the context of your focus. What you pay attention to doesn't matter as much as the type of attention you pay. If your focus on something is negative, you are materializing negativity. If your focus on something is positive you are materializing positivity. This is why it's called "paying attention." When you pay for something that is an exchange or transaction. You are getting a good or service for your money. In the same way when you pay attention you are getting something, hopefully of equivalent exchange, for your focus.

Emotions

The Law of Attraction is a universal law. It simply states that like things attract. Those like things attract because of the frequency at which they vibrate. This can be referred to as a flow. The flow of things isn't to be misconstrued with the flow of life. Life has its own vibrational frequency, but life also has a perceivably built in randomizer. You can't control life. Colloquially one might say, stuff happens. That unpredictable nature of life, at least in part if not in whole makes it uncontrollable. Things and or concepts can be manipulated because while they may evolve over time, they generally retain a certain amount of stability and form. Things are more rigid than life, and life is more fluid than things. You can flow with the flow of life as mentioned earlier, but that flow isn't the same flow as connecting yourself with various elements of life. The flow of life is the flow of things, but the flow of things isn't the flow of life.

Depending on your frequency you can flow in the same flow or frequency as the thing you want to attract into your life. Everything has its own flow or frequency. This is referred to as the Law of Vibration (reference back to chapter two). Focus differs from this (the Law of Attraction) because it's more concerned about your thoughts and uses how you're flowing (vibrating) as a point of reference. The main regulator of your vibrational frequency is your emotions. The way you change your flow or frequency is through how and what you emote. The Law of Attraction uses your emotions to influence your vibrational frequency, so that you can vibrate at the same wavelength as the thing you want to attract into your life (you can't attract the objective concept of life into your life, you experience it. Life is what it does. But you can learn to go along, traverse (or flow) with life). Your mind uses your emotions as a lens or frame of reference to help you interpret what your physiology is experiencing. Where your emotions radiate and reside is where your focus or centralized attention is located from a perspective of understanding. You'll understand something in a certain way based on the emotions you're using to associate with that thing. And where your attention is so is your consciousness.

Consciousness

Consciousness is the byproduct of what happens when an experience encounters one of your brain's chemical reactions. The human brain has a plethora of neurotransmitters. Neurotransmitters are chemicals released in your brain as a response to neural activity (the activation of your nervous system). When life affects you sensorially, your brain and nervous system through electrical signals called nerve impulses, make a determination about what you're experiencing and decides what to do about it. This is called integration in neuroscience and during this process after your brain draws a conclusion about that sensory input, neurotransmitters begin to travel across your synapses. Synapses are the terminals or means of connection between one neuron and another. As neurotransmitters travel from one neuron or nerve cell to another, they result in you producing a behavior or reaction. That resulting behavior/reaction is a direct result of the workings of your prefrontal cortex and hippocampus, among other parts of your brain.

The reason your prefrontal cortex can aid in your decision making is because it regulates your thoughts, working memory, attention, cognition, action, and emotions to name a few [executive] functions, by connecting with other parts of your brain. Your hippocampus is the part of your brain that concerns itself with memory, specifically episodic memory. Your brain takes new and stored information about various experiences and amalgamates that knowledge to generate decisions and behaviors. Your consciousness is critical to your focus because for all intent and purposes what you're actively responding to is a result of your attention being centralized towards something.

Attention and consciousness are effectively one in the same. Understanding this should make you at the very least more prudent about what you give your attention to. Because once you realize that the what of your attention matters less than the type of attention you're giving that what, the natural rational response is to give less or more thoughtful attention to various "whats." In laymen terms don't mentally pay for something you don't want. Or if it's something you do want, pay the mental price.

Energy

Emotions, behaviors, and reactions in general produce energy. Human energy is energy that humans exert. Humans get their energy from the molecules in food. Humans take that energy then we go do stuff like read and write. Whatever you do with your energy sends that energy out into the world. Energy doesn't disappear it translates or takes on different forms. When your energy translates from you in the form of centralized attention (focus) you are allowing that energy to manifest itself in a different medium. The means through which that manifestation takes place is a conduit. How you focus on something matters because of what will manifest on the other side of that focus.

The conduit being the mode of translation means, that your focus within the context of a conduit will produce something in relation to though not necessarily the same as that conduit (translations aren't always one to one or direct, but they are typically of relative equivalence). Take money for example. Objectively speaking money is not real. Money is a made-up construct that plays off individual, societal, governmental, and global buy-in to have a perception of being real. This perception is given objectivity based on the rules created around money (central banking practices, tax codes, inflation etc.). This results in money being seen as a store of value. The paper notes in your wallet or the digital numbers in your bank account mean something to you objectively based on government regulations, and subjectively based on personal sentiment. When you spend your money on something you are trading the value stored in your monetary notes for the value stored in some good or service. The value didn't disappear, it took on a different form.

Transportation, Translation, and Manifestation

The same thing happens with your energy. There is a direct positive correlation between focus and manifestation. Regardless of content or conduit, if you focus positively, positive things will manifest. If you focus negatively, negative things will manifest. This is how your energy is transported to a conduit. Your emotions send frequencies out, transport to, various mediums or conduits, or concepts or things. And those mediums translate those emotions allowing them to manifest or materialize.

If you only focus on what you're focused on, you're missing the power of focus. Change the perspective of your centralized attention and in addition to being attentive to what you focus on, focus on how you focus on what you're focused on. Altogether this process looks like giving your attention to something, receiving from that something whatever it's giving back to you in return for your attention, processing or thinking about that thing you got back for your attention, assigning an emotion to it, and doing something about it based on previously acquired experience. This is the constant cycle of consciousness that makes your focus valuable.

The next step to this would be intentionally emitting your thoughts and emotions about a thing towards that thing (vibrating). When you can vibrate on the same frequency, in the same way as, something you want, then you are engaging in the Law of Attraction, by purposefully connecting or flowing with the molecular and cosmic vibration and harmony of a thing. The result of focus and the Law of Attraction are the same, manifestation; but the final product, what manifests can differ greatly due to intentionality; and focus happens more automatically.

It can be common for people to negatively focus on something that they don't want in their life. Let's say for example you're upset at something, and you don't want that something to occur again. If you're like the average person you may focus your attention negatively on that thing and exert negative energy. This usually materializes in you acting out, saying words that are adverse or pessimistic, and or you experiencing symptoms of depression. The typical thought around behaviors like these in the presence of undesirable circumstances can be that if you rebuke that situation and circumstance enough, it will stop happening. What tends to happen instead is that, that negative energy you send out uses that situation or circumstance as a conduit to manifest itself in a different capacity.

What this looks like is, instead of that drama going away it either metastasizes into other areas of your life, or it gets caught in a negative feedback loop, and you end up reliving the situation continually because all your negativity did was produce more negativity. In this scenario the better thing to do would be to apply a positive focus to that experience and seek to learn and get something beneficial from it. That positive energy would use the same situation (conduit) and manifest itself in a way that you would probably find value in and appreciate more.

Humanity

Ultimately you give your context meaning. It doesn't really matter how something is objectively because it's still your job to relate to that thing regardless. Things are bad because you act like and say that they are. Things are good for the same reason. Be objective about your experiences and hyper-subjective about your responses. Focus on what you want to get from paying your attention to something. And if you decide you don't want anything from the thing asking for your mind currency, don't give it to it.

Additionally, how you treat people still matters. Don't use this as a license to ignore people because that's energy that will come back to you too. It's better to tell someone or something you're not interested in a polite and respectful way than it is to solely act like it. Your words are a more effective form of communication than your behavior. People can understand and interpret your words more easily than they can the nuance of your body language or nonverbals. And if you disrespect someone with your body language you may just be paid back in the same manner. Respect people's humanity because you don't know what someone is capable of. Walking past someone just gives them clearer aim at the back of your head. Use the totality of your mind's capacity to effectively communicate and will into existence the results you value and want for your life.

CHAPTER 24

Dynamic Thought

In life you must be able to think differently. Or at least be able to perceive other perceptions and perspectives. Everyone doesn't think the same as you, and that's a blessing. Growing up I used to think that the world would be a better place if everyone thought like I did. The only problem I had with that is too much of the same thing is annoying. I don't like "yes people." Yes people, are people who at least present themselves as not having thoughts of their own, or if they do, they aren't articulate or knowledgeable enough to voice their opinion.

Individuality has always been my jam. So, within that context you can see the trouble I may have had with wanting everyone to think like me, while at the same time being a big proponent of individualism Ultimately individuality is the greater inclination of people in the world at large. While there is safety in numbers you fundamentally can't rely on a group to have your personal best interests at heart. The masses are commonly referred to as sheep from the perspective of generally being easy to manipulate. The reason for this isn't that people all have the same thoughts, it's that they aren't all always encouraged or equipped to utilize the depth and breadth of their mental capacity.

People tend to not be conditioned to be individuals in a healthy way, just like they tend to not be socialized within the context of a society in a healthy way. That kind of free-thinking flourishes when you do what some may refer to as break out of the matrix. This means buying out of conformity, allowing yourself to see things more objectively, and making decisions and drawing conclusions based on that objectivity. The good news about people being independent thinkers is that they can contribute different and various kinds of thoughts and perspectives to a conversation or idea.

This is how you grow as a person, and how people grow within the context of society. It's the free flow of ideas that contributes to advancement and ingenuity. One of the pitfalls in this is that other people also understand this to be true. And not everyone is for your edification or the edification of people in general, let alone various people groups. Justice is justice. When you have knowledge, you can comprehend right from wrong.

If right is always right no matter what, that means if enough people are educated on an issue, they in their own capacity can draw objective conclusions on what is just versus unjust. That being said however, there are forces in life that may not want you or people in general to know the truth. The Bible tells us that the truth will set you free. Freedom is not an economic driver.

Let's take the history of black people in America for

example. Black people were brought to America as slaves to work the land and cultivate wealth for their white slave masters. As a byproduct of black people's labor, America has been one of the world's wealthiest nations. If black people were free sooner in America's history, or not brought to America at all, this likely wouldn't have been the case. Black people were extorted, brutalized, ostracized, demonized, and killed to build a nation. One of the ways in which this was done was by not allowing black people to be educated or to educate themselves. Black people in that particular period of American history, weren't supposed to know how to read or do math. One of the main if not only reason you don't educate people is to keep them oppressed and desolate. And oppression and desolation typically only benefit the oppressor and desolater. Your ignorance is someone else's gain economically or otherwise.

It's also an easier means by which you can be controlled and manipulated. There are people, places, and things that want to capitalize on your ignorance. There are also some instances where you may not want to know the truth. The human mind is really good at rationalizing, almost to a fault. This attribute however lends itself to our survival. That being said, your sense of survival can be weaponized against you either by yourself, or someone else, where you may choose the thing that is false, because it brings less turbulence than the truth. That's destruction and deception through relative peace. What you get for this kind of thinking and subsequent behaviors isn't worth what it costs. You commit philosophical suicide when you do this. You invalidate your own life. Ignorance isn't necessarily bliss and bliss isn't always that good to or for you. The concept of the lesser of two evils is a false dichotomy. Sometimes you must choose to struggle for the truth and for your freedom. Mental warfare is real.

Ideological warfare is real. The person that doesn't stand for something will fall for anything.

This is the value in having the perceptions of others and cultivating diverse thoughts for yourself. Being able to see things from various vantage points can contribute to you being able to see the whole picture, or at least a fuller one. You can't get your mind right if you're not willing to consider opinions that you may not hold to be objectively or subjectively valid, reliable, or sound. If everyone thought the same the world would be inherently less meaningful and less explored. It's the diversity of thought that fills in the proverbial blank spaces of life. And this matters because you are alive to live, and you can't truly live if you're not able to derive meaning and explore.

CHAPTER 25

Feature Not a Bug

What you go through is there to shape you. I can recall at the beginning of my sales career being told to "fire clients." The idea behind that is, just like you want to have clarity in terms of the kind of people you do want to work with, you also need to have clarity in understanding the kind of people you don't want to work with as well ("kind of people" in this case refers to people who demonstrate various certain types of behaviors). Even earlier in my life it was said to me that, the good thing about knowing what you don't want to do, is that you know what you don't want to do. In the formative years and seasons of your life you may not be able to comprehend that, some of the negative things you go through aren't just misfortunes, but rather they are purposeful misfortunes, not a bug but a feature.

Exposure is one of the best things you can get in life.

Having friends, forming relationships, and exploring life for yourself is valuable because it can curate vision. Sometimes the struggle people have with better is that they don't know what better looks like. The way you gain a personal understanding of what better looks like for you, is to see how good, better could be. It's hard to believe for a yacht if you've never seen or been on one. It's difficult to know what kind of exotic car you like if you don't know the kinds of exotic cars that exist. You can have trouble creating a meaningful and fruitful lifestyle for yourself when you're surrounded by toxicity (these are examples demonstrating sentiment and aren't necessarily representative of your personal interests).

This is the battle of your better: the knowledge of your experiences versus the knowledge or a lack thereof of what your life could be. All you have to do is have a suspended unbelief subjectively realistic vision (an unincumbered stretch goal that you believe could be possible in your life) of and for yourself, for you to make it happen. You or other people may say what can't be done because no one in your sphere of influence or yourself, may have ever seen or experienced anyone achieve a certain level of success firsthand. But here's the thing, you don't have to experience it to believe [for] it. You just have to be exposed to it and then want it bad enough to pursue it. Exposure doesn't have to be firsthand experience. Being introduced to a new thing or concept without necessarily having a sensorial encounter, can ignite a fire within you in and of itself. Sometimes the idea of a thing is enough to make you want to pursue the experience of it.

This is the value in letting your experiences inform your reality. The "bad" things in your life can serve the purpose of giving you something to hope for. Your potential doesn't mean anything until it's directed. Sometimes you need direction before you can direct. Having a concept of better through being exposed to new things can give you what you need to self-determine a direction for your life, ideally one that resonates with your desires being materialized in a healthy way. Once you have direction you can direct your potential in that direction, ultimately, becoming self-actualized. This also resonates with the idea of justice. By determining and acting on what would be objectively better for your life and or your corner of the world, you impose your will on and participate in lowercase "j" justice.

All of this is dependent on you knowing what better is. The challenge I find with concepts like good, or better, is that they are subjective. I don't feel as though it's my place to tell you what good or better is. I want you to know that better exists, period. I want to encourage you to pursue better and help you understand what behaviors and mindsets contribute to better. But ultimately you must decide the kind of person you want to be and the kind of improvement you do or don't want to see. There are adjectives and behaviors that are associated with people, places, and things that classify as being either "good" or "bad." I amplify the adjectives and behaviors that are associated with the "good" classification. Where you are or want to be on that spectrum, is on you. I want to expose you to what that spectrum is, what each side is like, and why I advocate for the good side. The practical way that this is informed and affirmed in your life is through your lived experience and specifically, sometimes through the unfortunate aspects of your lived experience. But if you can lean into those misfortunes, you'll see that they are actually a blessing in disguise. If you want to you can make that obstacle a breakthrough to get you closer to your compelling future, and or for the materialization of the concept of justice.

The good news about trials, struggles, and difficulties

is that they also build character. You can pursue your desires and do so with character and maturity. And when you accomplish something from a place of having developed character and maturity, you're more likely to have a greater appreciation for it. The reason you may have missed out on something good in your life in the past, is because you weren't mature enough to recognize or keep it. Your desires wouldn't have been placed in you if they weren't meant to be fulfilled through you. Sometimes what's required for that fulfillment is maturity and character development.

Another variable that presents itself in this equation is time. You may feel as though you don't have enough time to accomplish what you want to, or that things aren't happening fast enough for you. While it's true you ought to have a sense of urgency, what's also true is that urgency without focus is fruitless. You don't want to be busy doing nothing. If you can get focused on what you want and work towards it relentlessly, your perception of time will matter less because you know you're putting your best foot forward every day.

One of the drawbacks of perception is scale. Scale is the degree at which you do something. For example, scale for a rapper looks like, being a rapper, most people have never heard of with only a small following, or being a rapper who is a global superstar. In both instances both people are rappers. One just has a larger scale (being known globally with a larger operation) than the other (only having a small following and operation). People will allow themselves to be deceived by scale. This (self) deception can be harmful whether your scale is large or small in size and scope. The degree at which you can accomplish something doesn't matter as much as your ability to do so in general.

People can be enticed by scale because the promise of scale is more and better results and easier operations and logistics, in execution if not in complexity. If scale matters to you and it's not out of a necessity to meet a demand, you're facing then it may be nefariously motivated (derived from vanity, pride, greed etc.). If your scale is larger than your capacity literally, ideologically, metaphorically, or otherwise, you could take being at a large scale for granted or put too much stock in that.

You could end up overextending yourself by means of either budget bloat (spending more than necessary), or by not effectively meeting the needs of your consumer base (those demanding or expecting something of you). Having more, needing more, and doing more, don't always function in a symbiotic way. Focus on executing and the scale will come. Sometimes you must start small before big things can begin to happen. But don't lose sight of what those big things could be. Usefulness in your capacity to be more dynamic is a virtuous aspiration, but the execution of that virtue must be virtuous itself.

What you go through isn't an addendum to your story. A story about how you got over something only makes sense if there was something for you to get over. A story about how you made it out of poverty only makes sense if there was poverty in your life. You beating the odds only makes sense if there were odds for you to beat. Your accomplishments are your story. How you become who you are is built from the ground up with your raw materials. Your raw materials are the proverbials of your life.

If you didn't have a lot of money for an extended period of time, that's your raw material. If you don't have a quality support system, that's your raw material. If you've ever felt alone and or misunderstood, that's your raw material. Success is taking those things and doing something with them. That's how you create an ideal life for yourself. That's how you experience the better that you want. Play knowing you're the underdog. Play knowing you're the favorite. The "hand" or circumstances don't matter, it's how you play. This is life: playing the cards you were dealt and doing so, well.

It's easy to get caught up in unfortunate misfortunes. And I'm not even necessarily suggesting that grit, determination, and or powering your way through are the best options. I'm suggesting you use what you have and make what you want (happen). Don't be upset that you don't have enough of something, pivot and find a way to get it. Don't just make the most of something either (though there is nothing wrong with that at times) because that can be depending on the circumstance, indicative of a slave mentality. Making the most of something suggests you can't get what you want. Get exactly what you want and use what you have to do so. That's the story. That's your true story. That's your potential if you want it to be. Embrace what you have because that is what you need to pave the path to your better.

CHAPTER 26

Got Will?

The past is the present, the future is now, and the present isn't real. Time is distance divided by speed. Nothing travels faster than the speed of light. By the time you see light that is your present but it's the light's past. However, the light still exists so there is no objective present except for a new perception of a current past. Light's ability to travel quickly over distance while still maintaining its integrity invalidates its present, because its present is always happening to something else (whatever is exposed to the light), while at the same time never happening in the past tense to itself. Light doesn't experience itself; it just is and continues to be. The present is a hereness. It happens in the now but now is always changing so the present is never around long enough to be meaningful, except through an expression of the past or something previously experienced. That isn't native to light.

By the time you see a light, that light is doing something else. You may be experiencing it "currently," but whatever it is has happened already from the perspective of the light source itself.

The future is now because the future is the next moment following something spoken or written (literally or transitively). In relation to light, it only exists in the now because it's always happening or shining. The light's past is when it goes out; but even that is its future because it took on a different form, the absence thereof. All of this matters in relation to time (however distance divided by speed is measured in any given equation or formula). You just entered the future in the form of reading this sentence, and when you finish reading this sentence it will be the past. And now the past is your present because here is another sentence, just a different one. But the present doesn't objectively exist because the future is always happening (this is another sentence, and another is on its way). Now extrapolate this concept to your life...

Time is relative and only exists because it's agreed upon. Universally, humans measure the phases of the moon, the location of the planets, and the earth's revolutions around the sun. This is where time comes from. A clock gives numbers to celestial occurrences for our own collective and relative understanding. Those numbers mean nothing beyond a means of communication. It's easier to say it's this or that o'clock than it is to say sunrise, sunset, dark etc., as measurements for changes in the day. Pragmatically age isn't real. What's real is death. Your biology deteriorates and dies. Age is a concept and the negative byproduct of measuring celestial occurrences. You wouldn't know how old you are if you didn't know what time it was.

The word "age" at best gives us a frame of reference for

death, and at worst gives us an excuse. If all you knew is that from an objective perspective your physiology experiences "advancement," you wouldn't need a schema for said advancement. Time dilutes your growth because instead of focusing on your physical capabilities, education, wisdom, autonomy, and things that indicate objective human progress, time diverts your attention to sun revolutions, which gives you an excuse not to grow. Your body is going to grow regardless. But if your mind, thought process and way of thinking, and your character, who you are as a person, isn't growing at a similar or greater pace, you will not get the fullest harvest (metaphorically) from the fruit of your anatomic maturation.

There are things that big humans can do that little humans don't have the capacity to. But if your mind can't perceive big things then it doesn't matter how "old" you are because you can't take advantage of your newfound capabilities that come with advancing in life. Or if your character isn't developed you won't be ready or able even if you are capable because you don't have what you need as a person to rise to the occasion. If to you or someone you know, age is profoundly important, I posit that you or that individual is still psychologically adolescent. At no point have I made a claim that growth and progress are a bad thing. Inherently it's the nature of life. Maturation serves the purpose of enabling you to contribute to the continuation of the human race. Selfishly it's lucrative for you to become a better person but the scale of that lucrativeness is in the purpose thereof (inherent virtuousness). If you want to get the most out of your life understand what being a mature and developed person means to you, and why that's important from a sphere of influence perspective. When you're better you can help other people get or be better, which in theory contributes to a better world, when everyone acts on their better-ness. This is crucial to understand because knowing how to perceive time less passively and what that means to you, can change how you interact with the world.

Act on time don't let time act on you. You may be waiting for your desires, but your desires are also waiting for you. If you want to manifest them, you must do so outside of the construct of time. Time is finite. Once it's done its done. And that's the lie the devil wants you to believe. If he can get you to run out of time in your mind, you will run out of time in your reality, because eventually everything dies... But nothing was originally intended to die in the first place.

God created everything out of his eternal nature. The devil tricked Adam and Eve to forgo their eternity to take hold of knowledge. Once Adam and Eve took knowledge for themselves, death entered the world. Now because of that biblical perspective, things are more sensitive to time. While potentially a radical claim it's relatively safe to infer that time only exists because death exists. No death no time because if nothing dies then you have no reason to measure how close or far away death is perceptively, relative to your life (which depending on how you consider it makes time and death an interesting concept from the perspective of, if all people were able to align on one accord would it be possible to will away death, by the virtue of mass psychological formation not acknowledging it as a reality? This doesn't mean pretending it doesn't exist or pushing it to the back of our minds, which people tend to do, and which I will go into next. I'm suggesting eliminating the concept altogether. People would just stop dying because no one collectively believes or thinks death is part of reality. Somethings are only real because they are made real. Is it possible that the collective will of humanity makes death real, and that if we weren't in some respects hyper aware of it or could make it vanish completely as a schema, then no one would die because we would delete the concept from our understanding? Just a thought). Conceptually time is valuable mostly from the viewpoint of this question, "how long do I have until I or something I value dies?"

Virtually everything is measured with death in mind to serve the concept of time (at least proverbially if not literally). Time is a distraction. Measuring time has made death insidious and removed it from the forefront of people's minds. This doesn't mean that the alternative should be you constantly worrying about death, but if people didn't have a tendency to push death into the back crevices of their mind (or could erase the concept from existence), everyone would derive more meaning out of life (because people would fundamentally have the capacity to live objectively better. Instead of waging war in a world where no one dies, people could use that energy to be constructive and innovative. Admittedly however, not being able to die wouldn't necessarily solve the morality issue people have (what it is and those who are versus those who aren't), which I guess is why things are the way that they are). Knowledge has given humans the ability to hide the thing we may collectively fear most, because it's inherently unnatural and counter to our original design. So instead of living time free we (humans collectively) measure time as a way to perceptually neuter death, because if we know what time it is, we can say, "I still have time." "Running out of time" isn't a real thing either, it's a placated way of saying you are being/have been lazy or lack in proactivity, or you feel as though you are dying.

The castration of death is the influence of Moloch because of its self-harming nature. If you can measure time, you can in your knowledge determine time as well. You know what 9am on a Monday means to you. You know what 9pm on a Thursday means to you. But if you can break out of that constraint, you'll see that time for all intents and purposes is not objectively real, and therefore is less detrimental on your life than you may be open to admitting. Not being constrained to time is freedom.

This matters because if you can will it, it's already done. Will is expressing the future tense. The future is the moment following something spoken or written, literally or transitively. Therefore, the future is always happening. If the future is now, and will is expressing the future, the question is, got will? Are you willing-ready, eager, and prepared, to express your now?

Your desires will start happening once you start making them happen. Your life has the opportunity to improve when you take action. Don't give time power over you. If you worry about time, you may miss or give up on your will. When the proverbial "it" happens doesn't matter in the slightest. What does matter is that "it" happens. Your desires wouldn't be placed in you if they weren't meant to be made manifest through you. You must be willing to act on your now which is the future. Tomorrow isn't promised so don't wait for it.

Tap into today, tap into here, tap into now, then do it. Your willingness makes a way for you. If you're just "waiting and hoping that one day…," you'll miss the version of what you are waiting for that you could be experiencing now. Now is cultivatable. What is now doesn't have to continue to be next. You can make improvements on your now when you work on it.

Dream about what you want, meditate on it, and align yourself with it. What must you do to get to the next check point of your life? What is the next check point of your life? The conceptual struggle of will is between knowing what you must do and acting on it. Don't worry about the how if it's for you, then it's for you. Now is immediate. You must be willing to do something in the immediate and then not just be ready or capable to do it, but also follow through and actually do it. I would argue that if you don't automatically take the action associated with your will, then you're inherently unwilling (there is a paper-thin delineation between willingness and action. You demonstrate your will through or with your action).

Faith is taking a step and not knowing if there will be another step in front of you. Faith is one of if not the only effective counter to the risks of life. Everything is risk but if you can have faith then the risk won't seem as risky (and doing nothing may be riskier). This is the bedrock of willpower. Start believing in that still small voice. Start believing in the positive proclamations over your life. Start believing in your affirmations. Be ready, eager, and prepared, and live in the now.

CHAPTER 27

Confidence

Confidence isn't always acquired, sometimes its discovered. Sometimes the only way in life is to support yourself. Confidence is, "with-fidelity." After everyone and everything else in your life falls short of what's required for you to excel, the final option is to have fidelity in and with yourself. You must support you. Sometimes that does look like being selfish. Sometimes that does look like saying "no" even though you could say "yes." Here's a little secret, the people, places, and things that aren't supporting you are already doing the same thing.

The noun that said no to you, probably could have easily said yes. The noun that used you for its personal gain or prioritized themselves over you, didn't lose a wink of sleep. Sometimes your self-support comes from looking around and seeing no one there. This is why getting your mind right is invaluable as it relates to you getting the most out of your life, because you need to be able to think clearly and make objectively good decisions.

The good news about autonomy is you don't have to behave the way other people do. You can break cycles if you so choose. Generational curses can be no more if that's what you want. Around the Covid-19 pandemic back in 2020 God placed me in a context where, all the relatively close people around me that I was paying attention to were buying homes, becoming millionaires in the stock market, and doing something with their life. Meanwhile, I was struggling to do anything of value with mine.

Around that time, I was laid off from work and the only "creative" thing I could come up with was to write. And frankly the origins of my writing didn't come from me desiring profitability. I am not a fan of self-exploitation. I started writing independently to express myself freely. I felt prior to doing so, that the nouns in my life didn't really care about my well-being and that whatever "kind" words they said were merely lip service. If I were to continue living for other people rather than myself, I would have probably taken my own life by now. The problem is when people use you so uncaringly, they don't care if you kill yourself either.

This is where the seeds of confidence for me were discovered. If the same things that make my life miserable don't care if I don't exist, then I don't need to give them the satisfaction. Your enemy wants you dead anyway. Sometimes you may be placed in situations where you look at the things around you, not in terms of comparison, but as inspiration. At the same time as the people in my sphere of influence were becoming "overnight" millionaires, I was beginning to have a vision for myself.

If I didn't see it happen for them, I wouldn't have been

able to see it happen for me. But then because I support and have fidelity with myself, I took it a step further and learned how to do it for myself. I come from poverty. Resourcefulness historically wasn't a strength of mine. Poverty can look like a whole host of things: no cash, no assets, no intellect, no will, no know-how, no righteousness etc. All the people that I felt inadequate around because they got their millions without any effort had more resources than me.

But what I lacked in resources I made up for in confidence. Even though it wasn't happening for me didn't mean it couldn't. Anything that God can't do doesn't exist. This is an immutable and theological, philosophical, and existential character trait and understanding about who God is. I believed. I believe. That was my way of rising out of obscurity. But I also had to learn that belief requires ruggedness. If you don't get anything else from this chapter, I hope you get that you need to say, "no" [a lot] more times than you ever say, "yes" from now on. And I pray that lesson sticks with you and you act on it every day. If you go six months only saying no, go another nine and a half years doing the same thing. Don't remove yes from your vocabulary but just know that most yeses aren't worth it.

Confidence comes in all shapes and sizes; you need to find the thing that makes you want to support you. What makes me want to support me is saying "no." If sometimes being confident looks like being an asshole, be an asshole. Supporting yourself is crucial because no matter how much help you get, if you're 18 years old or older you're an adult, and no one wants to take care of an able-bodied adult. Get your money and go, believe in yourself when no one else will, say no with a straight face to loved ones, friends, and family, and put your phone on do not disturb and or block contacts. Live how you are meant to live.

Make the devil mad and go be happy. When you get to where you're supposed to be don't go back to where you're not. Even if that means you have to die on the streets in a foreign land. That's better than dying in a palace because someone you know holds animosity towards you. This is my experience, find your equivalent and govern yourself accordingly. Take your second, third, or whatever number chance you're on, and don't need another one. Become sane. Don't do the same thing over again this time. You know how that story goes. They don't love you; they don't even know what that word means. Free yourself.

You're waiting on Jesus and Jesus is waiting on you. Leave house, leave home, leave family, leave friend, and don't go back (Matthew 10). Whatever you need to do to support you, that is where your confidence is. That is where the meaning of your life is. After you finish getting your mind right, get your life right. Act on what you know. The only way knowledge becomes power is if you do something with it. And the good news is, once you break the bad cycle(s) in your life you can proliferate your success. You can't make someone else do better, but you can help them know what better is. Give your life meaning. *You* get better not bitter.

No one truly has your best interest at heart, because at the end of the day everyone worries about themselves. In the wild, animals either eat their offspring or push them out into the world and maybe not even hope that they make it on their own. Humans are just smart animals. If you don't make it on your own you will be eaten by things close to you, society, and or whatever powers that be in your life. Create the life that you want to live then live it. There is nothing wrong with wanting to be and do more. Find the confidence required to do so. If you can make your life mean something, then it will. Comprehending life isn't as difficult as you may want it to be, you just may not like reality.

CHAPTER 28

Manor

In 2022 I was evicted from my apartment. I was late on my rent because money was being difficult to come by in that season of life for me in a novel way. It was the tail end of the pandemic, the end of the federal eviction moratorium, and I was coming up on the end of my lease. I wasn't intentioned either way as it relates to renewing my lease or not, though I probably would have. My landlord said to me in no uncertain terms that she could evict me, get someone else to move into my apartment, and charge more money for it.

Profit was the motive. Even after a miraculous string of events where I was able to acquire the funds necessary to remain in my apartment, instead of holding off on exercising the court granted eviction, the landlord exercised their right to kick me off their property expeditiously. The problem at the time was, I wasn't inclined to be homeless.

What I mean by that is I became relatively comfortable with the notion of homelessness, however, I concluded that was not the life I wanted to live. What this white, Christian-cross-wearing woman, possibly with a family of her own, may or may not have known was, she was effectively conducting a societal execution and borderline neo-lynching on me.

I am not inspired to drag anyone in the mud, I am just opining on what I, on the other side of organizational greed and profit exploitation, have experienced and been exposed to. Why might I invoke such strong language as it relates to my being evicted? Well, white supremacy is the underlining ideology that rules the system in which I, a black man, am subject to in America. White supremacy is white preservation at all costs. The DNA of a white person is genetically recessive. In America in particular, to protect and preserve their numeric majority, white people must castigate minority races; none more so than black people who are the original people and have dominant DNA traits.

Evicting me and having such a demerit placed on my credit report with an outstanding balance sent to collections, was a blatant example of white supremacy consciously, subconsciously, and or unconsciously, affected upon me. First of all, it can be a challenge to have an eviction removed from a credit report. Secondly, renters are super not interested in entertaining an evicted person's futile attempts to find somewhere else to live. I had access to monetary notes via the job I got literally on the exact same day as my eviction hearing. But my social cachet via my trustworthiness represented by what was not a 750+ credit score at the time was basically eviscerated. Losing your ability to be taken objectively seriously if not relatively so in a society dominated by covert and overt white supremacy, as any person of color, is for all intents and purposes a virtual assassination.

I was a victim of what is the desired end goal for all non-white people in a white supremacist system, death and or disenfranchisement. This becomes more feasible to comprehend when you're confronted with the fact that, during this happening to me, I was also told that previous/other tenants of the property were shown leniency and allowed to be late on their rent. All this is framed in the context of prior to the moment described, I was never delinquent by the grace of God.

God caused it so I wouldn't find meaningful work between before and after I was evicted. I can't make this up. This was after exhausting my savings and looking for a job for months. Having somewhere to live was not in the cards for me, at least not at the time. The situation exacerbated even more when the job I was blessed with didn't contribute to assisting me in being able to make and save enough money to pay the eviction off and have it removed from my credit report.

When I am faced with such a challenge as the one being described I can't help but think of the overall purpose and implication for my life. God had no will for me to stay in that apartment or for me to be able to get into another one anytime soon. Why? Well, you know they say you can ask God any question except for why, otherwise you'll be inundated with a wave of platitudes that don't pacify the root of the question. For what purpose did God want me to experience homelessness?

Well for one, had I not had this experience this book probably would be different or not exist at all. But then I think about my ambitions, and I wonder... Because as I've laid out, there are a multitude of things wrong with capitalism as an economic system, and I've learned since this experience that not a lot motivates me. I've known this in the past however, in the past I thought it was a problem and that I needed to be overzealous about something and have a cause. That was inauthentic to me but what I thought was the right thing to do; to care.

Since the turmoil of this chapter, I don't really care about much. I don't value money as a motivator. Being poor or coming from poverty and desiring money or having it as a motivator, when all it does is depreciate, is an example of what God referred to in the Garden of Eden as a slow death. You're dying in real life, and while you're doing so you're also wasting your time chasing after something that doesn't mean anything.

I won't go too far into my personal thought process on this however, as someone who values so little to the degree that I find something to be worth my labor, and while still wanting to manifest my desires and not live on the streets, I had to rectify within and to myself the point of striving for anything in the first place.

The conclusion I came to is, when you don't have anything or anything else to live for, live for yourself. Every now and again you must do things for you. Not selfishly though that is the nature of this point, but rather in a way rooted and guided by morals and convictions. When you have responsibilities of a certain kind you can feel inclined to capitulate on your values. It's easier to endure hardships when you have someone relying on you to show up and follow through almost every time.

But when no one appears to be on your side from your mild assessment, you have nothing materially to live for, you don't necessarily care about the repercussions on the people in your sphere of influence, you have no dependents, and every day you learn more and more to make your peace with death, of which the Bible calls a benefit, you can find yourself in the interesting position of asking, what do I have to live for that I actually care about?

If this is relatable to you then the answer to that question must be yourself if it isn't already. Owe it to yourself. Be your own cross in Christian terminology. Jesus literally died for all of humanity, you can die for yourself metaphorically. Endure the struggle every day for you. You can't let the enemy win in difficult times. What if God's will for you is for you to will a meaningful life for yourself? Create what's not given to you. Make meaningful and lasting relationships. Enjoy what's meant for you to enjoy. No one is perfect and all beliefs are liable to have a gray space for the subjective. But that's the whole point. Sometimes the best and only thing you can do is live out your subjectivity to the fullest and hope and pray that's enough.

If you're going to risk anything, risk having a life. Do the hard thing. Not having a life is easy, life is already setup to be robbed from you by the ruling systems. If you can't have your ideal life, at least have one to the best of your ability that is rooted in and guided by your morals and values. If you don't stand for anything you'll fall for everything. Live a moral life. Live an objectively good one. It doesn't have to be and probably won't be a perfect one, but it should be yours. Do the unquestionably right or correct thing that also doesn't make you a foot note in your own existence. Don't live for anything that doesn't inspire or encourage you to get out of bed in the morning.

Sometimes when you go through certain hardships you can become jaded. I've been building a business and brand since 2019. At the time my efforts weren't producing money. It can be really easy to give up when you aren't seeing what you want to see and or you feel stuck in an inescapable situation. Sometimes those types of hardships aren't present because of a lack of resources, but rather they are a byproduct of the intolerance of the systems of this world.

I believe the Judeo-Christian God is the God of everything. This belief has put my relationship with him in a precarious position on occasion. Every good and bad thing comes from God, directly from his heavenly throne room. Even the devil still takes marching orders from God. But if you are a believer then that means you believe that God is good as an immutable attribute. If God is good, and he allows or causes bad things to happen to you, then there can be cognitive dissonance within a person as it relates to their understanding of the word "bad" and what bad is. In some cultures, colloquially, bad can mean good.

When I look back on my life and think about personal hardships, various difficulties with various nouns and systems closely present in my life, being poor, being evicted, having bad credit, my business endeavors not producing the results I wanted when I wanted them, having to take jobs that I didn't want to participate in a society that is at best ambivalent to my success, and at worst diametrically opposed to it, and being confronted with giving up on my goals and desires, and I put all that in perspective with "God is good;" that tells me that there may be something wrong with what I want.

If all those things I've listed are actually good things, then what is the good thing? They all must add up to something...

Manor is the name of the city I lived in almost immediately after I was evicted. I was able to find a room to rent for a while. I sometimes still reflect on that time. Having to be out of the house Monday through Friday. Riding public transportation to work every day. Watching myself be unable to save money. I didn't have the resources to eat healthy food. I had to scrape by. When you fight for something harder than that something is willing to fight for you, then you should probably change what you're fighting for. The American economic structure has not worked for me. Being profit driven has not been my savior. I don't and didn't want to be poor, but I needed to create my own path and my own definitions for things. American capitalism wasn't coming to my rescue. To that system if I made it great, and if I didn't, even better.

CHAPTER 29

The Value in Adding Value

What if I told you that the fastest way for you to start making more money, is by making money the least essential part of what you do and why you do it (whatever it is that you do)? The common denominator when it comes to successful businesses and individuals alike, is their ability to provide as much value to others as possible. How much you give is correlated to how much you receive. This does not mean that by giving away all your money, you will automatically double the amount in your bank account. That is a delusion.

What's real is that all of us are given what we are appraised at. The question is, who is doing the appraising at any given juncture in your life? When you agree to go to work to build someone else's asset(s) for 40 hours a week for example, the salary that you agree to do that work for, is the appraisal that is placed on you filling the role. Three things are at play in this example: One, the role itself has value in terms of what that role means to whomever is looking to fill it. Two, you have value in general but also in terms of how the person hiring for said role values you in that role. And three, someone else has value in general and also in terms of how the person hiring for said role values them in that role.

A director position can start at $100k a year, while another position in the same company may have a starting salary for much less. This isn't because there is a world of difference between the two people in those contrasting roles (not including maybe education and experience which is a fair subjective distinction in this scenario). But there is a world of difference in how those two roles are valued, and how the person or people filling that role value the potential candidates for that role (one example of this that you may have encountered or will encounter is something called "cultural fit." Cultural fit can be one of the many non-quantifiable and subjective ways that a person is valued.)

How Do You Value Yourself?

Objectively each one of us has an evaluation, or how much we could potentially contribute to any given scenario. It's your responsibility to operate in a value equals money mindset as opposed to a time equals money mindset. The difference is in how/if you allow someone else to appraise you.

Money isn't real. Money is a vehicle that allows you to be a productive and contributing citizen in a society. Before and after you become a cog in a corporate machine or something similar, you are a soul. This means that your true value is not in what you can do but rather it's in who you are.

You add value to people and to the spaces and places you inhabit when you live out your passions. If you want to lead a meaningful and wealthy life, you can't compromise on your passions.

Western society specifically not exclusively, has favored the citizens thereof being appraised by what they do rather than by who they are. When you switch from a time equals money mindset to a value equals money mindset, you start placing a higher value on yourself. You become more valuable from the perspective of having a better conception of what you're capable of. You'll be inclined to work towards becoming more valuable. An average job has you doing something you may not extract any meaning from naturally ("meaning from naturally" meaning in a way that edifies you and not just puts money in your pocket).

When you value yourself, you'll look to find things that will improve your skills and abilities, and that will make you and what you do more meaningful not just to yourself, but also to the people you do what you do for. Valuing yourself makes you instantly more valuable because in part it means you put a standard in place for yourself. You won't be as quickly inclined to say yes to everything that comes your way.

What is Value?

Frequently value can be found being equated to profit in capitalist societies. Profit is financial gain. Its money left over after overhead expenses. Value is intrinsic worth or usefulness. Capitalism put broadly, and or corporate structures, can fall into a tendency of valuing profit and profitability. The issue with this thinking and ideology is that who you are only matters in more cases than not in these circumstances, in relation to how much you produce-and not necessarily for yourself. Within the context of a business/business environment the way you flip this dynamic on its head is by making profitability an outcome and not an input. You don't need to make x amount of dollars or convert x number of prospects into clients by the end of quarter whatever. You need to generate x amount of value that will produce x amount of revenue/desired results based on such and such conversion metric(s). You not reaching your revenue goals is not your frequent repeat customers' problem. Find out why your return customers return and do more of that.

Creating a surplus does not give any one individual a virtuous endowment. As a human, like all other natural things on earth, you already come with endowed virtue. No one has to tell you or make you feel valued or valuable, the value is already in you. When you get your mind right you tap into what's already (possibly lying dormant) inside of you. This is one of the reasons why I say that your desires wouldn't be in you if they weren't meant to be fulfilled through you. Desires are eternal. You don't have to want something; the something you want is already impressed upon your conscious. Your job is to want to materialize *that* something.

How bad do you want to do whatever it is that you want to do with your life? That's value. No one assigns that to you. No one can measure that in wages. Someone can inspire it in you, but your value as is most value (objectively speaking), is intrinsic. Yet and still if it's intrinsic then that means it's subject to subjectivity. The struggle that value has when competing with profit is that value is too abstract to substantially influence the profit motive. An employer can care less about, sometimes to the detriment of the company, the value a person or a feature brings if they aren't also bringing in two to five times more profit in relation to said value.

That's like you being a great employee rhetorically. Your co-workers like you, the mail person for the office is friendly with you, your managers think highly of you, but you don't "wow" anyone in your execution. All of what makes you pleasant doesn't have to be/isn't required to fundamentally matter when put in contrast with profit margins. Even if those ancillary things make a notable impact on production as a whole (i.e. your nice demeanor and disposition motivates those around you to perform more/better).

And here is where subjectivity gets complicated, because under such circumstances it's up to you as an individual to decide with a certain level of sobriety, what objectively matters to you personally; and what is worth your labor. This can be referred to as "going against the grain." The grain doesn't work for everyone. The grain didn't work for me. Timing and seasonality are worth mentioning here too, because sometimes certain things working more or less in your favor are dependent on where you are contextually in your life.

It's not the grain's fault that you don't work well under its conditions, but it is your fault if you don't find something for yourself that does work for you. Real value is knowing and acting on what's worth your worth and disengaging with that which isn't. And while you may not make [a lot of] money for it, if you can have the courage of your convictions in relation to how you value yourself, you'll live a more meaningful life.

I want to drive this point home because I'm not saying that your only choices are to be miserable or be poor. What I am saying is if going with the grain is not worth what's required of you to do so, don't do it (literally, metaphorically, proverbially, or otherwise). But also know that just because it's not worth it to you doesn't mean it's not worth it to someone else. And the job of you determining your value is deciding how much your life means to you. Your value is only as valuable as you make it; and you demonstrate that by deciding to do something with your life that also doesn't capitulate on your morals and convictions.

If you complain about your job every day, are constantly stressed out, wish you were making more money, feel stuck in your current role, or even just wish you were appreciated more for the work that you do, than it is safe to say that maybe you are not being properly valued; mainly by yourself but generally by any party involved in the perpetuation of the aforementioned feelings.

What's Your ROI?

I can relate to this point because I had to figure out how to appraise myself for what I felt I was truly worth, and not for what someone else said I was worth. This was multi- faceted and in all areas of my life. I had to consider the advice of friends, my education and experience, what I wanted for myself, and my willingness and potential among other things.

(As an aside, not everyone cares about what you want for yourself. You could be talented and have several deals inked and happening. You could have the car and the mansion, but if someone doesn't consider you with or value you having those things, they won't perceive you with them. It's like a hater saying you can't do something, meanwhile you're doing exactly what they said you couldn't do right in front of their face. In fact, you invite them to watch you do it, and they still say you can't do it. They have blinders on. They either can't see or don't want to see you doing it, even if you're literally doing it right in front of them. They don't care about what you want for your life, they only care about hating and being a hater.

Haters who only care about hating are like that because putting you or someone else down gives them value and meaning. They don't want to get better or see you in a better light, they want to use you as a punching bag to make them feel better about themselves. It's sad because they are unhappy in some aspect of their life and supporting you is an affirmation and confirmation to them that they won't amount to anything [more]. Not caring about or encouraging you wanting something personally significant for yourself is how they retain validity for themselves.)

I learned to live in such a way where it became impossible for me to allow myself to be undervalued. The best way to determine your own value is by measuring how much value you give to someone else.

Return on Investment (ROI) is a key indicator for how an investment is doing. The goal of an investment (spending commonly money, or some other like asset for the purpose of gaining profit) of any kind is to see a timely return greater than the value of that which was initially spent. This can be applicable to every aspect of your life. The value equals money mindset puts you in a position to constantly ask yourself: how valuable am I holistically?

That does not mean, "how much money do I have in the bank?" Again, money itself is valueless. What makes money valuable is what you do with it. It means, how are you proliferating whatever it is you have to offer in a meaningful way?

Are you giving back? If so in what capacity, and/or can you do more? If you can hone in on doing something meaningful for someone else that is life affirming and not life draining for you, the money will come; and that's the whole point. When you're doing something truly valuable in relation to who you are as a person, money will become second nature as a byproduct of your value, and not the thing that makes you valuable in and of itself. Think bigger.

The Value of Adding Value

Look at large companies like Amazon, Microsoft, and Apple. They each have large market capitalizations, but why do you think that is the case at its core? Because they all provide a tremendous amount of value to their customers. You don't need to be a business to add value. You don't need to be attached to a business to be valuable. Effectively all you need to do is be an objectively good person. Regardless of what you do for a living, you must be able to honestly conclude for yourself if whether you are providing tremendous value to or with your work, and or to/for the people in your life.

Do people know how reliable you are? Can people call on you for the big project to be completed? How trustworthy are the products and services that you offer, and does what you do closely align with who you are? When you merge your passions with your values you start living with purpose. Purposeful living is more rewarding and gratifying than all the money in the world.

When you live on purpose that means you are living the life you are meant to. When you live on purpose you can't help but to be a servant to others. The golden rule is to do to others as you would have others do to you. Put another way, serve the way you want to be served; and impact the lives of others the way you want your life to be impacted. This is how you add value and how you identify your own value.

Living with Purpose

From a theoretical standpoint you want to add value to other's lives because you want to actively engage with the Law of Reciprocity; the idea that what you put out in the world comes back to you on a mutual standing. This correlates with the Law of Value which states that the amount of value you receive commonly in the form of money but not exclusively, is proportional to the amount of value you put out into the world (products, goods, services, support, intentionality, etc.).

The more "good value" you put out into the world the more "good value" you receive in proportion, and the same goes for the opposite. The practical value in adding value is scalable. What do you get from adding value to a person's life and to what degree? Who are you adding value to, and what does that value objectively mean to the recipient of said value? For a business or business minded individuals this could look like being seen as trustworthy and an honest broker. Allowing yourself or company to build name recognition and familiarity. And or being able to expand your capabilities to more people and or markets.

For Life with Ken as well as myself as example, one of my tenants that I try to live by to a certain degree and transmute into my work is to be as supportive as possible. I know well what support and or a lack thereof can mean for the trajectory of a person's life. My compassion and understanding for this contribute to what influences my personal and professional instincts.

As a purposeful individual you may seek to add value because it gives you the room necessary to grow and develop. As well as advance in life, positively impress upon people, and it can give you the ability to create and leave a legacy for yourself. The goal is to realize that we all are more valuable than a dollar amount associated with an hour of time. The same thing that gives a CEO value is the same thing that gives a janitor value-the fact that they are souls.

When you become effective at touching more souls, your bank account will become more effective at attracting more money. Who you are is mor important than what you do. And what you do should be influenced by who you are. It is not about what you do at face value. It's about why you do what you do and who or what you do it for.

CHAPTER 30

The Now of God

God can make a way when there seems to be no way. Can is an interesting word in reference to God. Can is an ability. The Bible says that God is able. Able doesn't mean obligated. Just because God can or is able doesn't mean that he wants to. This is referred to as the will of God. What is God willing to do for you? What are you willing to do for God?

If you can will it, then it's already done because will is an expression of the future and the future is now. Is God doing anything for you right now? Whatever is happening to you right now is the will of God for your life. Typically, it's not God's long term will that people can have difficulties with (of which people tend to placate by saying things like, everything will work itself out). It's his immediate will. What does God want for you now, at 2pm on a Saturday? Or at 6pm on any given Monday? Now.

One of the best things you can do for yourself is have a positive relationship with now. Now is always happening. Now is an amalgamation of consciousness and the passage of time. But it's not something you experience it something that happens. Now represents the present which isn't real because here comes the future. Now is the moment at which the current future happens and turns into the next future. It's a subtle experience but that is where anxiousness can live because now is so ambiguous. What's now right now doesn't have to be the same now in the next now, which is now.

Part of life is about learning to trust God in the now. Frankly I don't think God wants us to know everything at any given point in time. God keeps things from Jesus. What we are to know God will divulge. What we don't need to know we won't know. There is power in understanding that your life, and life in general is on a need-to-know basis, and that you don't always need to know.

One of the many good things about God is that he's consistent. If your current now either on a macro or micro level is boring, then it's a good bet that it will remain that way at least for the next few "nows." I heard it said in a videogame once that boring is a good thing. Boring is a good thing because boring implies stability. Nothing dramatic is happening. There is no big emergency or life change taking place every other moment. It's like a ship on calm waters, steady as she goes. That's God's desire for you and me. For our proverbial ships to be steady as they go.

Don't worry about what God can do. Knowing that he can do anything is purely for the benefit of your knowledge. It's information that you should know as it relates to you having hope as you go through life. Betting on what God can do will likely result in maybe not so favorable results, because when you focus too much on the can you can miss the is.

Learn to be appreciative for what God is doing. Because what he is doing is what he wants to be done.

CHAPTER 31

Get it Off Your Chest

Every now and again a moment may come along in your life where you are granted an opportunity to speak your mind. All the work you do/have done professionally, personally, emotionally, physically, intellectually, psychologically, relationally, or otherwise will be useless and moot, if in that moment you don't garner all that experience to be dignified and purposeful. Once you've gotten your mind right, rise out of obscurity. When it's your time, it's your time; own your time.

Time is such an interesting subject because of its multifaceted-ness. In this instance in reference to time I am referring to the moment when you are the expert in the room. When you are under the spotlight. When you are given the mic literally or metaphorically and asked to express and elaborate on your take, on any given matter or topic. Your opinions and perspectives are not free. They come at the cost of your privacy and anonymity. Generally speaking, a society wants to know if you have thoughts. It doesn't necessarily care about what those thoughts are. Your personal information, whatever it is, serves someone else's profit motives.

Your mind is one of if not your most powerful weapon. Thinking in a way that is clear for you comes with things that are personal, fun, exciting, depressing, shameful, and or exhilarating. It's your job to pick and choose your words carefully. Don't allow yourself to be robbed by an experience thief (someone who wants to use your experiences and personal stories for their own gain). Understand what the moment calls for and speak to that. One of the deceptions of living in the 21st century is feeling as though your business is everyone's business. It's not.

The reason to get your mind right in the first place is to position your life in a way that is suitable for you. For a long time I lived my life for other people and not for myself. Then I came to a place where living for myself for a myriad of reasons became the right thing to do both subjectively and objectively. The messed-up part was, I knew that I should've been living for myself even while I wasn't doing so. I didn't have the courage of my convictions to say something. I was being too sparing of other people's feelings, while being left on multiple occasions holding the proverbial bag.

I was afraid to stand up for myself. And the people around me knew my business (or so they thought), but they didn't know me. And that's because they didn't want to know me. To them I was more useful than substantial. Some people may refer to this as being the "scapegoat." As a youthful individual I knew to speak my mind, but I was concerned with stupidness like, what if that person/those people don't like me anymore? What if I get into a fight? Or what if I get that person upset with me? And this is the point that I'm making: nobody cares.

You're not as valuable to the people who make you feel valuable pretend you are. *You're not as valuable to the people who make you feel valuable pretend you are...*

What I was experiencing and what you may be or have been experiencing is a toxic relationship. You may have or had more than one in your life. A toxic relationship can take form in any context where two or more humans share the same space for whatever reason (notably you can also have a toxic relationship with yourself depicted by how you speak to and treat yourself). It's emotional drugs. The people who manipulate you know how you like to be manipulated. And the people whose feelings you're sparing know that you're sparing their feelings.

One of the most insightful things that someone once said to me was, "they know how they treat you; they know what they are doing." The Bible says to not throw your pearls to swine. When you find the courage and have the moment to put on display and demonstrate your growth, progress, and maturity, make it a showcase. A showcase is when someone exhibits their talents and abilities. Sometimes development can only be demonstrated to be appreciated. And sometimes that demonstration and appreciation is only for yourself; for you to see how far you've come, and not for you to prove yourself to someone else. Stop perpetuating what you don't want in your life. Be willing to do the work to discover and or face the facts of what it is you don't want. When a significant moment for you comes, don't behave foolishly when people are literally, metaphorically, or proverbially waiting with bated breath for what you're about to say and or do. And don't disclose anything that you don't want to.

Acknowledgements

Jesus, Maxie, Tracy, Crystal, Allie, Rebecca, Raven, Tonya, Jessica, Shay, Morgan, Sophia, and Destiny. To my future being better than my past. Education, camaraderie, fermented drinks, and eggs cooked multiple ways. To baked wheat and spreads for said baked wheat. Real good authentic olive oil. To proliferation. Synonyms. The Life with Ken community. Almost everyone and anyone at any period of time who has helped me with content production of any kind. And to being in tune with nature and the comfort and authenticity that comes with that. This book is the result of an amalgamation of all the aforementioned. I want the post publishing of this book to be a soft reset for me to be as awesome as I can be. Positivity only.

This book marks a period of time for me that was, but now it's time to step into what is and what is to be, not just for me but for you too. Know better do better. Become the subject matter expert of your life. Be free, be confident, be you. 100%. Nothing less than yourself. And don't let a loser stop you. If someone has something to say about you having a revelation about a life worth living for yourself, they are a loser. Give them a copy of this book. Or just disassociate/create space from them. Somethings require moments to pass for healing to ensue. Get healed. Help others get healed. Learn from moments and let them pass.

About the Author

When I first wrote this part of the book I did it in third person, but I want it to be more personable. My name is Kenneth Wyche. I am a lot of different things. My faith is important to me, it guides and informs what I do, but what I am passionate about doing is helping you get more out of life. I arrived at this place because of the immense empathy I have for the misguided and ill-informed. I wish to provide credible information and experiences that can transform your life. When you do better everything around you does better.

Some people choose not to get better for that exact reason, because they don't want the people, places and things around them to improve as well. My life journey so far, in this era of my history, has been about coming to terms with unfortunate realties and making decisions to create something better. This book highlights what some of that journey has been like and provides you with some information and context that you could potentially use to create something more fulfilling and meaningful for yourself. For more from me you can visit https://www.lifewithken.com. Thank you.